the brokea$$ gourmet cookbook

the brokea$$ gourmet cookbook

by Gabi Moskowitz

Dynamic Housewares

EGG&DART™

EGG & DART™

Published by Egg & Dart™, a division of Dynamic Housewares Inc

First paperback edition of 2012

Author: Gabi Moskowitz

Book Design: Chris Lorette David

Copy Editor: Kerribeth Mello

Manufactured in the USA

ISBN: 978-0-9838595-1-2

For Jeremy.

table of contents

In early 2009, a recession hit America. Hard. Every day I heard from another friend who had just lost his or her job. My city, San Francisco, home of a bazillion start-ups and tech firms let go of hundreds of thousands of employees. Suddenly, we were all BrokeAsses.

I started to notice an interesting trend: These friends of mine, who had had good jobs, all got used to making comfortable salaries straight out of college. They worked 80-hour weeks developing the next great search engines and video games, ate corporate-catered meals at their desks and had little time for friends . . . or doing other things like learning domestic skills. When that bubble burst, they found themselves hungry . . . and too broke to feed their newly-developed champagne tastes.

This got my friend Adam Metz (an internet marketing consultant and absolute genius) and me (a kindergarten-teacher-turned-caterer) thinking . . . what if we teach these people how to cook in an easy and inexpensive way? What if we show them that it doesn't require a whole lot of money or skills to eat as well as they had been before they were broke? He had the web know-how and I had the food and writing skills, so together, we built BrokeAssGourmet.com, which we hoped would become a tool and source for our starving and kitchen-inept friends. Every recipe, we decided, would cost less than $20, for the whole thing. None of this "Well, it's $4.83 per serving. . . ." business. If you have to buy a jar of nutmeg to make a BrokeAss recipe, I'm not going to try to tell you that you're only using $0.03 cents worth of nutmeg. Times are tough and you might only have $20 in your checking account—so if you're going to need to drop money on a whole jar of nutmeg to make a recipe of mine, you're going to want to factor that into your food budget in advance, which is why I'll include the cost of the whole jar.

I also wanted people to understand the crucial-ness of having a well-stocked pantry. How cooking becomes little more than picking up a few fresh ingredients when you already have the flour, olive oil, salt, pepper, etc. A basically stocked pantry means you can stretch out a week's worth of groceries to maybe a week-and-a-half or two weeks, if necessary—you just have to be prepared.

And booze! Just because you're broke doesn't mean you can't drink well! It's just a matter of choosing wisely and learning a few little tricks. Inexpensive wine, beer, and cocktails, we decided, would have a presence on Brokeass Gourmet as well.

More than anything, we wanted to help people understand that even though they might be low on funds, they can still live the good life. It just takes a little thoughtful planning and the development of some really basic skills.

chapter

1

getting started

In my book (and, I mean, this is MY book, so I guess I'm speaking both literally and figuratively), the ability to cook is high up on the list of grown-up skills that everyone should have, regardless of gender. Having a clean, well-stocked kitchen and essential kitchen tools on hand are the building blocks of producing tasty, healthy meals that don't drain your checking account. That is, after all, the whole point of all this, right?

Here's a little-known secret: Cooking is easy and even a whole lot of fun. More fun than going to a restaurant, in my humble opinion. Even if you've never done it before. Even if you're kind of afraid of your stove. But, like anything, if you dive in unprepared, you are not likely to meet much success, which is where I come in. With a few good tools, techniques, and ingredients, you can be cooking great food, saving money, and impressing your friends (and that cute boy or girl you've had your eye on too . . .).

So read on for a step-by-step, anyone-can-do-it guide to readying your kitchen (no matter how tiny—and I know tiny kitchens!) and yourself--no frilly apron required (but, I mean, if you like frilly aprons, I'm not going to stop you).

step 1: clean

Having a clean kitchen makes cooking significantly more enjoyable. Food keeps longer in a kitchen that is free of mold, bugs, and mice (gross, I know, but more common than you'd think), and such parasites stay away from clean spaces. It's also much easier to clean up little messes when your kitchen itself isn't a big mess. A clean kitchen is easier to acquire and requires less than you might think. You'll need:

- **2-3 sponges (1 for dishes, 1 for counter, 1 for scrubbing)**
- **Multi-purpose cleaner**
- **A broom**
- **A mop**
- **Paper towels**
- **Dish soap**

Take everything out of your pantry/cupboards. Go through each item and determine if it's (a) still good and (b) something you'll ever eat. If it's neither, toss it; if it's both, keep it. If it's still good but you'll never eat it (and it's unopened), donate it to your local food bank. If it's been opened but you'll never eat it, attempt to pawn it off on your friends/roommates, but if you're unsuccessful, toss it.

Before you put all the dry goods you're keeping back on their shelves, use the abrasive back of a wet sponge to scrub all the grit from the shelves. Once the grit is removed, spray them down with multi-purpose cleaner and wipe away and put back the dry goods you're keeping.

Do the same thing with your refrigerator and freezer.

OK, you with me? Good! Now it's time to go shopping!

step 2: shop

To really succeed in the kitchen, you'll need some well-made basic kitchen tools. There's no need to go too fancy, but remember, you'll be using these things over and over again, so make sure to purchase quality, simple products. Got it? OK, great. Now go hit Target or a good restaurant-supply store (These places are the best! You can find amazing deals.) and pick up the following: a rubber spatula (for scraping), a medium-sized balloon whisk, 2 or 3 wooden spoons, 2 sturdy plastic cutting boards, a large chef's knife, a serrated knife, a set of mixing bowls, a rolling pin (hint: a wine bottle can stand in in a pinch), measuring spoons and cups, a large frying pan, a soup pot, a smaller pot for sauces, and a couple of nonstick baking sheets. Bonus items include an immersion blender, a food processor, a cast-iron pan, and a grill pan.

OK, are you with me? Cool. Now it's time to buy food.

step 3: stock

Head to Trader Joe's or your local grocery store and fill your cart with the items below. For around $50 you can fill your shelves with dry goods that will make cooking easier and less expensive because you'll already have many of the ingredients on hand.

Note: Whenever you see "Pantry" referenced in a recipe, I'm referring to ingredients you should already have in your $50 Pantry. Prices are approximate.

The $50 Pantry

- **unbleached all-purpose flour (I prefer King Arthur)** | $4 for a 5 lb bag

- **extra-virgin olive oil** | $6 for 12 ounces

- **vegetable/canola oil** | $4 for 16 ounces

- **kosher salt** | $3 for 24 ounces

- **pepper (ideally in a grinder)** | $3

- **baking soda** | $3 for a 6-ounce can

- **baking powder** | $3 for a 6-ounce can

- **white granulated sugar** | $3 for a 16-ounce box/bag

- **brown sugar** | $3 for a 16-ounce box/bag

- **honey** | $4 for 8 ounces

- **balsamic vinegar** | $4 for 12 ounces

- **peanut butter** | $4 for 12 ounces

- **mayonnaise (store it in the fridge after opening!)** | $3 for 16 ounces

- **garlic** | $0.50 for a head

As for fresh ingredients, resist the urge to buy out the entire grocery store. Pick up a few basic perishables (eggs, milk, butter) that you use regularly, but otherwise, wait until you have decided what to cook before you spend much on meat or produce. If you plan your meals and shop for meal-specific fresh items, you will save money since you'll actually be buying less and because you won't do things like buy a beautiful steak you fully intend to cook, but then forget about until it's gone bad.

Now that you've got your kitchen under control, it's time to move on to the bar. Don't worry if you don't actually have a bar in your house—a well-stocked liquor cabinet and a kitchen counter will do just fine.

the basic budget bar

Hosting impromptu parties is a whole lot more fun when you already have the beverages on hand. With just a little good planning and some smart shopping, you can be mixing fancy cocktails in no time—all in the comfort of your own home and for less money than you think.

I typically buy mid-range liquor brands for mixed drinks, reserving higher-priced top shelf liquors for the occasional times when I drink sans mixers. Here's what you'll need:

Liquors/Cordials

- **Vodka, Gin, Light Rum** | $12–$15 for 750
  The building blocks to nearly every cocktail—and the most versatile spirits to have around, making them extremely cost-effective.
  Recommended brands: Seagrams (vodka and gin) and Castillo (rum)

- **Brandy, Whiskey, and Bourbon** | $13–16 for 1 liter
  Not as versatile for cocktail mixing, but essential for hot drinks like Hot Toddies and Irish Coffee
  Recommended Brands: Paul Masson (brandy), Evan Williams Black (whiskey/bourbon)

- **Triple Sec** | $6–9 for 1 liter
  If you're going to buy a cordial, buy triple sec. Seriously. When it comes to mixed drinks, it is the single most-used liqueur.
  Recommended Brands: Aristocrat, Arrow, Hiram Walker

- **Other Cordials** | $5–$12/ 750 ml
  Buy these in small bottles—they're typically very sweet and a little goes a long way. Some of the most popular flavors include: peach, raspberry, melon, amaretto, and sour apple. You may not use them often, but they're great to have when the craving for a specialty cocktail hits.

Now that you're stocked, it's time to get mixing. Here's a basic formula for cocktail creation. My friend Laith, a bartender at San Francisco's Hobson's Choice calls this cocktail template "The Monkeyspanker." I'm not sure why, and honestly, I'd rather not know. I just thank him for his drink-creating brilliance and move on. Seriously though, use this as your cheat-sheet when mixing drinks and you'll never go wrong. I even have a copy of it taped to the back of my liquor cabinet!

the monkeyspanker

PREP TIME: 0:05

ingredients

2 parts main liquor (i.e.: vodka, gin, rum, etc.)

1 part cordial/liqueur

3 parts juice or other mixer

Ice and fruit garnish, if desired

directions | Makes 1 drink

Just add ice. shake (stir, if using soda). and pour into glasses and garnish.

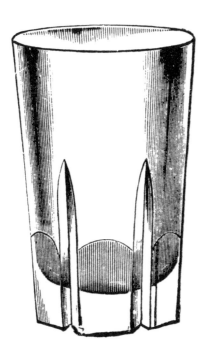
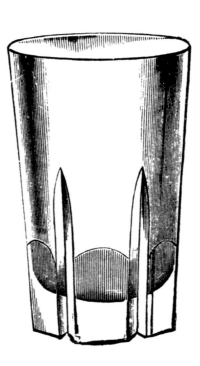
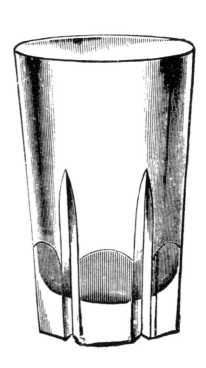

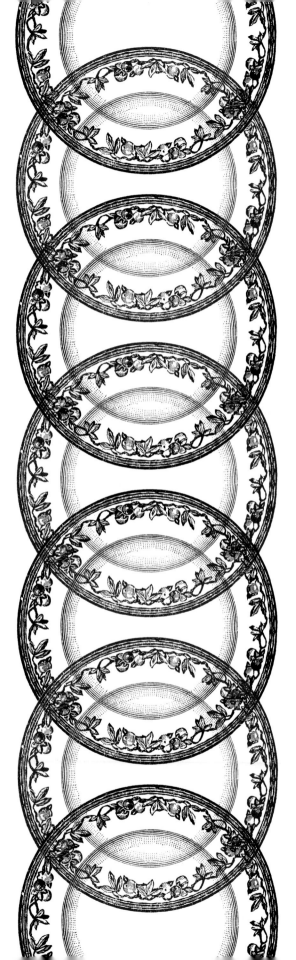

chapter

2

drizzle, dip, dollop

Learning how to make your own dips, dressings, and sauces is a giant step in two great directions. First of all, while it can be tempting to buy these things ready-made, store-bought condiments are typically pricier, more sugar-and-preservative-laden, and less tasty than homemade ones. Once I learned to make my own salad dressing and figured out how cheap, easy, and delicious it was, I ceased buying bottled dressings altogether. Homemade dressings are a simple way to kick up your salads to instant gourmet fare. Secondly, in many instances, once you've made your sauce, you're more than halfway to eating. Did you just whip up a pot of fresh tomato sauce? Just add some inexpensive cooked pasta and it's dinner time. Is that a batch of guacamole in your hands there? Bring on the chips and suddenly you're the most popular boy or girl at the party. Peanut sauce, you say? Just add rice noodles and some shredded carrots.

I bought a cheap set of mason jars at my local hardware store and use them over and over again for homemade dressings, sauces and jams. Also, come the holidays, add a pretty label to jars and give them away as thoughtful, unique, and very inexpensive to make gifts.

peach-jalapeño mustard

This one is not for timid tongues. (Isn't "timid tongues" a great phrase? I got it from Didi Emmons, author of Vegetarian Planet.*)*

The cool, sweet peach and soothing honey meld with the jalapeño and Dijon, resulting in a pleasantly hot chutney-esque sauce that I think is just amazing with spicy bratwurst. If you wanted a sweeter, mellower sauce, you could definitely use honey mustard or regular yellow mustard in place of the Dijon.

PREP TIME 0:30 | COOK TIME 0:15

ingredients | Total Cost $5

2 teaspoons extra-virgin olive oil | Pantry

¹/₂ onion, finely chopped | $0.50 for a whole onion

¹/₂ large peach (white or yellow) | $0.75 for a whole peach

4-5 tablespoons dijon mustard | $3.50 for 8 ounces

few grinds of fresh black pepper | Pantry

1 teaspoon honey | Pantry

1 medium green jalapeño, seeded and finely chopped (leave the seeds in if you like it hot) | $0.25

salt (if needed) | Pantry

directions | Makes about ¹/₂ cup mustard

1. Heat the oil in a small pot over medium-low heat. Add the onion and cook for 8-10 minutes, allowing to caramelize.

2. While the onions cook, bring a small pot of water to a boil. Place peach half, skin-side-down into the boiling water for 45-60 seconds, to loosen skin. Rinse peach half under cool running water, then carefully pull off the skin. Dice peach and add to the caramelized onions.

3. Turn the heat up to medium and cook the onions and peaches together for 4-5 minutes, until peach breaks down completely. Remove from heat, transfer to a clean bowl, and refrigerate until mixture reaches room temperature.

4. To the peach-onion mixture, add the mustard, pepper, honey and jalapeño. Stir well, adjust seasonings to taste (I didn't need salt, but if you do, add it now).

5. Store in an airtight container until ready to use (up to four days).

fresh caesar salad dressing

I once had a spectacular Caesar salad at the now-closed Pesto Café in Sebastopol, CA. The owner (who also served me) promised that I wouldn't be able to stop licking the bowl because the dressing was so good—and she was right. As I raved about its deliciousness, she shared the secret ingredient with me—ginger. It seemed strange, but I couldn't argue with the addictiveness of the salad dressing, so I decided to give it a try. Here's my knock-off—it's pretty darn close.

PREP TIME: 0:15

ingredients | Total Cost $9

1 clove garlic, smashed | Pantry

3 anchovy fillets plus more for garnish | $2 for a 2-ounce tin

1 egg yolk | $1.50 for 6 eggs

1 teaspoon minced ginger | $1

juice and zest of 1 lemon | $0.50

¼ cup plus extra-virgin olive oil | Pantry

⅛ cup shaved Parmesan, plus extra for garnish | $4 for 10 ounces

salt and pepper to taste | Pantry

directions | Makes ½ cup dressing

1. Combine garlic, anchovy fillets, egg yolk, ginger, and lemon juice and zest in a blender or food processor. Pulse until smooth.

2. With machine running, slowly stream in ¼ cup olive oil until dressing is very creamy and thick. Add Parmesan and pulse until dressing is slightly chunky but well-combined, about 45 seconds. Season with salt and pepper to taste.

classic balsamic vinaigrette

This dressing is as simple as it gets, and works well with many different kinds of salads. Toss with mixed greens, shredded carrots and croutons, for a simple, bistro-style house salad, or add chopped egg, crumbled goat or blue cheese, avocado, and grilled chicken for a lighter take on the Cobb salad.

PREP TIME: 0:05

ingredients | Total Cost $0

1 clove garlic smashed | Pantry

¼ cup balsamic vinegar | Pantry

⅓ cup extra virgin olive oil | Pantry

1 teaspoon honey or sugar | Pantry

salt and pepper to taste | Pantry

directions   Makes about ⅔ cup dressing

1. Combine all ingredients in a bowl. Whisk with a fork until emulsified. Use immediately or refrigerate, leaving garlic clove in dressing until ready to use.

creamy yogurt-herb dressing

My friend Rachel orders a side of ranch dressing with just about everything—way beyond salad. It doesn't matter what is in front of her—she believes that nearly every food item is improved with a little drizzle of the creamy stuff. She laughs at my grimace as she happily swirls her sushi (or pizza or hamburger or spaghetti) in it.

While I normally subscribe to the school of thought that fresh salad greens need little more than a little good extra-virgin olive oil and something acidic, such as balsamic vinegar or lemon juice to be palatable, I do see ranch dressing's place in the world. My version, made with yogurt and olive oil instead of mayonnaise and buttermilk is light yet satisfying. Pour it over salad, or, if you're like Rachel, whatever you want.

PREP TIME: 0:05

ingredients | Total Cost $4.50

1 cup plain yogurt (whole milk or low-fat) | $2 for a quart

1 handful fresh basil leaves | $1 for a bunch

1 handful fresh cilantro or parsley leaves | $1 for a bunch

juice of 1 lemon | $0.50

2 cloves garlic, peeled | Pantry

pinch each of salt and pepper (more or less to taste) | Pantry

$^{1}/_{8}$ cup extra-virgin olive oil | Pantry

directions | Makes about 1¼ cups salad dressing

1. Puree all ingredients in a blender or food processor. Store in an airtight container (a mason jar works well).

balsamic fig jam

Figs are a big favorite of mine. Once, in the middle of winter, when figs were out of season and I was feeling deprived, my friend and fellow fig enthusiast, Sue, suggested I get my hands on some fig jam. I thought that sounded like a good idea, so I decided to make my own. The result was something that tempted me to dip a spoon into its jar every time I open the refrigerator. Try it with bread, cheese, and prosciutto, swirled in oatmeal, or on a sandwich with almond or peanut butter.

PREP TIME 0:05 | COOK TIME 0:25

ingredients | Total Cost $4

1 pound dried figs (preferably Black Mission), ends removed | $4

¹/₂ cup balsamic vinegar | Pantry

2 tablespoons honey | Pantry

pinch of salt | Pantry

directions | Makes about 1¹/₂ cups jam

1. Combine all ingredients in a saucepan. Add ¹/₂ cup water.

2. Cook covered, over low heat for 20-25 minutes, until all liquid is absorbed and figs are very soft.

3. Puree using a blender, food processor, or immersion blender.

4. Allow to cool before serving.

roasted tomatillo salsa

Roasting a fruit or vegetable is a great way to bring out its natural sugars—and the tomatillo is no exception. This salsa has a lovely, versatile texture and is perfect over chicken or fish. Personally, I prefer it with tortilla chips and a cold beer.

PREP TIME 0:05 | COOK TIME 0:25

ingredients | Total Cost $5.50

3 regular tomatillos or 6 small ones, husk intact | $1

4 cloves garlic, peeled | Pantry

1 jalapeño, seeded and halved | $0.50

1 small white onion, peeled and quartered | $0.50

3 medium tomatoes, any type, quartered | $2

1 small bunch cilantro | $1

juice of 1 lime | $0.50

salt and pepper to taste | Pantry

directions | Makes about 1½ cups salsa

1. Preheat oven to 475°F.

2. Spread tomatillos, garlic, jalapeno, onion, and tomatoes on an ungreased baking sheet. Roast for 20-25 minutes or until tomatillos are soft.

3. Remove tomatillos from their husks and place in food processor or blender along with the other roasted vegetables and all remaining ingredients. Pulse to desired smoothness.

4. Serve with chips, burritos, tacos, or over meat, fish, or chicken.

homemade mayonnaise: a love story (sort of)

The first time I made mayonnaise from scratch, it was a disaster. I gathered the ingredients for a batch of fresh, rich, egg-yolky, olive-oily, lightly lemony mayonnaise. I didn't follow a recipe, I simply combined the fresh ingredients in a bowl and set about whisking until my arm felt like it was going to fall off. Despite my efforts, however, twenty minutes later, I found myself with nothing more than a useless mess of oil and egg yolk. The problem, I surmised, after finally deigning to read a recipe, was that I had added the oil too quickly. Instead of very slowly streaming it into the bowl of egg yolks in a thin and steady stream, I had glug-glugged the oil in choppy increments, beaten the bejesus out of the mixture, then added more oil, and repeated the process. I had been overzealous and careless and there was, it seemed, no saving my would-be mayonnaise.

So there I was, holding a bowl of "broken" mayonnaise with a very sore arm. I thought I might cry.

I was, however, fiercely determined to unbreak my mayonnaise. So I went back to the aforementioned recipe and reviewed the "tips" section. To recover a broken mayonnaise, it said, place a teaspoon of water into another bowl and then add the broken mayonnaise drop by drop into the water while whisking, just like you added the oil to the egg yolks before. When you have incorporated all of the broken mayonnaise into the water, slowly add the remaining oil (if any) while whisking, just like before.

I had nothing to lose, so I did as the article said, exercising caution as I poured the oil-and-egg mixture from a spouted measuring cup, drop by drop into the tiny pool of water. I whisked and whisked and, lo and behold, a thick, creamy sauce eventually began to form. It seemed like an eternity before I poured the last few drops out, my wrist aching from holding the cup at such an awkward angle, but by the time I finished, the result was a velvet-smooth, pale yellow sauce—totally different from (and far tastier than) store-bought mayonnaise.

I scraped most of it into a jar to be stored in the refrigerator, and stirred a few tablespoons together with some minced garlic, fresh herbs, and paprika to make a perky aioli to serve with sweet potato oven fries.

And so, I learned, some things can, in fact, be unbroken provided you exercise a little creativity, restraint, and perhaps most importantly, the willingness to try again.

PREP TIME 0:25

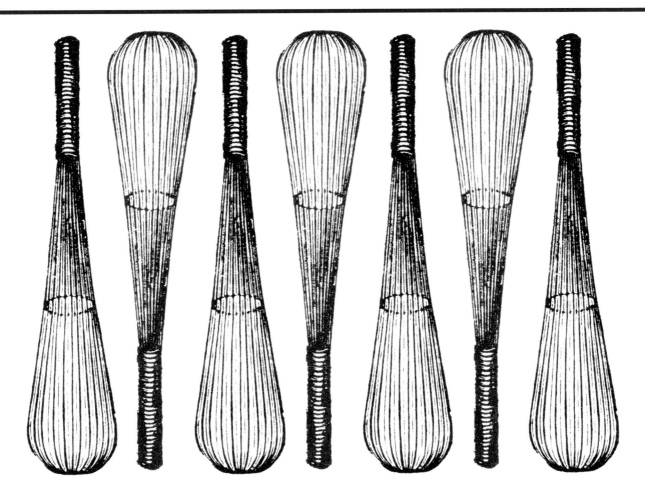

ingredients | Total Cost $2

3 egg yolks, at room temperature | $1.50 for 12 eggs

juice of 1 lemon | $0.50

1¹/₂ cups extra virgin olive oil | Pantry

salt and pepper to taste | Pantry

directions | Makes about 1¹/₂ cups mayonnaise

1. Whisk together the egg yolks and lemon juice in a large bowl. Very slowly, whisk in the oil, pouring it in an extremely thin, steady stream. This should take several minutes. A thick creamy mayonnaise will form. Season with salt and pepper to taste.

fresh pico de gallo

The easiest salsa recipe ever. For quick guacamole, simply stir this into a couple of mashed avocados.

PREP TIME: 0:20

ingredients | Total Cost $6

7-8 firm Roma tomatoes, diced | $3

½ medium white (or yellow) onion, finely diced | $0.50 for 1 onion

2 jalapeños (remove the seeds for less spice), finely diced | $0.50

1 large handful of fresh cilantro leaves, chopped | $1 for a bunch

Juice of 2 limes | $1

salt and pepper to taste | Pantry

directions | Makes about 2 ½ cups salsa

1. Mix all ingredients together. Serve with tortilla chips, or with tacos, fajitas, or burritos.

peanut sauce

This is one of those crazy-good, lick-the-bowl sauces. Everyone will beg you for the recipe. You, like me, will be the queen (or king) of the potluck when you serve this with spring rolls, dumplings, or even sweet potato fries.

PREP TIME 0:10 | COOK TIME 0:00

ingredients | Total Cost $7

¼ cup peanut butter (creamy or crunchy—your choice) | Pantry

6 ounces coconut milk | $1 for a 6-ounce can

1 small bunch cilantro, cleaned, stems intact | $1

2 cloves garlic, peeled and smashed | Pantry

1 small piece ginger, peeled and chopped roughly | $0.50

2 tablespoons soy sauce | Pantry

juice of one lime | $0.50

1 tablespoon rice vinegar | $2 for 10 ounces

1-2 teaspoon(s) Asian chili sauce | $2 for 8 ounces

1½ tablespoons honey or brown sugar | Pantry

directions Makes about ¾ cup peanut sauce

1. Combine all ingredients in a food processor or blender. Adjust spiciness to taste by adding more or less chili sauce. If the sauce is too thick and needs to be thinned out, add a little hot water. To make into peanut salad dressing, increase the rice vinegar to ⅛ cup.

fresh tomato sauce

This recipe was invented one evening after I had gotten a sweet deal at my neighborhood's farmers' market on heirloom tomatoes. They were just five dollars for five pounds of slightly soft organic heirlooms—perfect for cooking with. I simmered them with simple ingredients and ended up with a sweet, fresh-tasting sauce, perfect for pasta, chicken, fish, or just dipping crusty bread in.

Hint: This easy, versatile sauce looks very pretty in mason jars, making it a great, inexpensive gift.

PREP TIME: 0:15 | COOK TIME: 0:30

ingredients | Total Cost $5.50

1 tablespoon extra virgin olive oil | Pantry

1 onion, diced | $0.50

6 cloves garlic, chopped | Pantry

3 pounds fresh tomatoes, cored and chopped | $3

1 large handful fresh basil leaves, chopped | $1 for a bunch

1 large handful fresh flat-leaf parsley leaves, chopped | $1 for a bunch

directions | Makes about 5 ½ cups sauce

1. Heat olive oil in a large pot over medium heat. Add onion and garlic and cook just until fragrant, about 1 minute.

2. Add chopped tomatoes, basil, and parsley. Stir and cover. Cook for 8-10 minutes or until tomatoes have broken down.

3. Puree, leaving the sauce slightly chunky, using a food processor or blender and return to pot. Or, use an immersion blender and puree directly in the pot.

4. Turn heat up to medium-high and cook, uncovered, for 15-20 minutes, or until sauce reduces to about ½ of it's original content.

5. Remove from heat and toss with pasta, spread on pizza, or serve with fresh bread for dipping.

orange-cardamom applesauce

Applesauce has developed a reputation as the least-sexy snack around, and for good reason. The prepackaged kind tends to consist of bland, runny pureed apples, sugar, and preservatives. Clearly, you're better off making your own, which is great because it's absurdly easy and has the added benefit of making your house smell amazing.

Try a spoonful swirled into yogurt or over sweet potato pancakes.

PREP TIME 0:25 | COOK TIME 0:35

ingredients | Total Cost $8.50

3 pounds good cooking apples (Granny Smith, McIntosh, Fuji, etc.), peeled, cored, and chopped coarsely | $3

Juice and zest of 2 oranges | $1

4 tablespoons honey | Pantry

1 teaspoon ground cinnamon | $1.50 for 1 ounce

2 teaspoons ground cardamom | $3 for 1 ounce

½ teaspoon salt | Pantry

directions | Makes about 6 cups applesauce

1. Combine all ingredients in a large pot with 1 ½ cups water. Stir well and cover.

2. Cook over medium-low heat for 30-35 minutes, or until apples completely break down. Use the back of a wooden spoon to gently smash the apple pieces once they begin to soften. Add more water if the applesauce gets too thick.

3. Let cool slightly, then serve warm. Alternatively, let cool completely and store in an airtight container or in mason jars until ready to use.

red wine-shallot seduction . . . er, reduction

I don't really like to cook for men I am dating (or trying to date), at first, anyway. For most people, "let's cook together" is code for "let me prove to you that I have mad care-taking, domestic skillz, and then let's make out on my couch." But I covered that part (the skillz part, anyway) when you asked me what I do for a living; you know I can cook—it says so on the business card I gave you when we met. And I totally do want to make out on your couch, but frankly, I have been cooking all day for work, and the last thing I want to do at night is attempt to keep my mascara from running while chopping onions and flirting with you. Let's just go out instead.

That said, dating me (or any food professional) is not without benefits. Once you have proven that your interest in me extends beyond my kitchen abilities, I will gladly tie on an apron (I'll wear a cute one, just for the occasion.) and make you a meal that will blow your mind. No, I don't need assistance—you just bring a bottle of wine and chat with me while I stir. (Also, I don't want to blow my chances with you by revealing too early my teeny-tiny little tendency to totally micromanage the way you chop garlic—trust me, it's better if you don't help.)

So here's what's going to happen. You'll arrive at my house with the aforementioned bottle of wine. Upon entering, you will smell the most luxurious, intoxicatingly delicious fragrance ever. You are going to fall in love with me just a little bit before you even get halfway down the hallway leading to the kitchen because the scent is just going to be that good. You'll come into the kitchen, where I will have some warm, crusty bread waiting (probably some Boucheron and a little fig jam as well), and farmers' market-fresh veggies ready to sauté in butter. I'll have a couple of steaks grilling and on the stove, you'll see the source of the heavenly aroma wafting throughout my apartment: a little saucepan of something magical. You will wonder what this aphrodisiac-in-a-pot is, and when we finally sit down for dinner and I spoon its contents over our perfectly grilled steaks you'll be blown away by my skills (skillz). You'll want to go make out on the couch right away, but I'm classy and so I'll at least insist we finish our dinner first.

And here's the thing about that good-smelling concoction: it's just a bunch of stuff dumped into a pot and cooked until it has reduced down to a thick, buttery, savory-sweet liquid. Also, it only cost me about four bucks.

Because, yeah, not only am I a really good cook, I'm awesomely clever, too.

PREP TIME: 0:05 | COOK TIME: 0:40

ingredients | Total Cost $4

3 tablespoons unsalted butter | $1 for a stick

2 shallots, finely chopped | $0.50

1 bottle inexpensive red wine | $2.50

2 tablespoons balsamic vinegar | Pantry

salt and pepper to taste | Pantry

directions | Serves 2–3

1. Melt the butter in a small pot over medium-low heat and add the chopped shallots. Cook for 7-8 minutes, allowing them to caramelize.

2. Pour in the wine and continue to cook for 25-28 minutes, until the contents of the pot are about ¼ what they were when you began. Add the balsamic vinegar and cook for another 5-6 minutes. Season with salt and pepper to taste and use (over grilled beef, pork, or chicken) immediately.

pesto 5 ways

If you have a food processor or blender, pesto is one of the quickest, easiest ways to add sophistication and a fully packed flavor punch to dishes—and it goes so far beyond the classic basil pesto you're familiar with. Here are five of my favorites, but feel free to experiment. After all, pesto is little more than the blend of an herb, a nut, an oil, and sometimes cheese. The possibilities are endless.

fresh basil pesto

Fresh basil pesto is one of those foods that you've probably bought prepared, but once you make it fresh you will find yourself making it again and again. Fresh lemon juice and zest brightens up the flavors and keeps your pesto tasting fresh for days.

PREP TIME: 0:05

ingredients | Total Cost $8.50

2 cups tightly packed fresh basil leaves | $2

$^1/_2$ cup grated Parmesan cheese | $4

$^1/_2$ cup pine nuts | $2

6-8 cloves garlic, peeled and ends removed | Pantry

$^1/_2$ cup olive oil | Pantry

zest and juice of one lemon | $0.50

salt and pepper to taste | Pantry

directions | Makes about 1 $^1/_2$ cups pesto

1. Pummel all ingredients in a mortar and pestle (add the basil gradually so it breaks down without creating a huge mess). Alternatively, place all ingredients except lemon juice and olive oil in a food processor or blender and stream in liquids as the machine runs. Process until you have a smooth paste.

lemon scallion pesto

Smear on fresh salmon before baking, serve with freshly chopped veggies for dipping, or toss with whole-wheat noodles and serve cold for a fabulous picnic salad.

PREP TIME: 0:05

ingredients | Total Cost $9

about 10 basil leaves | $2

6 scallions | $2

6 garlic cloves | Pantry

¼ cup grated Parmesan cheese | $4

¼ cup olive oil | Pantry

juice and zest of one large lemon | $1

salt and pepper to taste | Pantry

directions | Makes about ½ cup pesto.

1. Pummel all ingredients in a mortar and pestle (add the basil gradually so it breaks down without creating a huge mess). Alternatively, place all ingredients except lemon juice and olive oil in a food processor or blender and stream in liquids as the machine runs. Process until you have a smooth paste.

creamy avocado pesto

This creamy pesto is indulgent without being overly rich, thanks to heart-healthy avocado and just a touch of olive oil. Also, since it uses a fresh avocado for its creamy consistency, rather than pricey Parmesan cheese, it's less expensive to make than traditional pesto.

It happens to be vegan, but don't let that deter you (if you're the sort of person usually deterred by vegan recipes)—it's fabulous, particularly with fresh heirloom tomatoes. I also like it as a dip for vegetables or slathered over grilled fish or chicken. Use soon after making it though, as the fresh avocado will go brown if it sits for too long.

PREP TIME: 0:05

ingredients | Total Cost $5

1 ripe avocado, peeled, pitted, and diced | $1.50

1 cup (packed) fresh basil leaves | $1 for a bunch

1/3 cup pine nuts | $2—buy in the bulk section

3 cloves garlic, chopped | Pantry

juice of 1 lemon | $0.50 for a whole lemon

2 tablespoons extra-virgin olive oil | Pantry

water as needed

salt and pepper to taste | Pantry

directions | Makes about 1 cup pesto.

1. Combine avocado, basil, pine nuts, and garlic in a food processor or blender. With machine running, slowly stream in the lemon juice, olive oil, and water as needed to achieve a smooth pesto. Puree until completely blended and creamy.

2. Season with salt and pepper to taste.

3. Use immediately or keep, refrigerated, for up to four hours.

rosemary-walnut pesto

Smear this earthy, nutty pesto on chicken before roasting, spread on baguette slices, or serve with sweet potato fries for a unique and delicious dip.

PREP TIME: 0:05

ingredients | Total Cost $9.50

¹⁄₄ cup walnuts | $2

2 large handfuls of fresh flat-leaf parsley leaves | $1

2 cloves garlic, peeled | Pantry

3 tablespoons olive oil | Pantry

leaves from 3 twigs fresh rosemary | $1

1 lemon, juiced and zested | $0.50

salt and pepper to taste | Pantry

directions | Makes about ¹⁄₄ cup pesto

1. Combine walnuts, parsley, garlic, olive oil, rosemary, lemon juice and zest, salt, and pepper in a food processor until a slightly chunky paste forms.

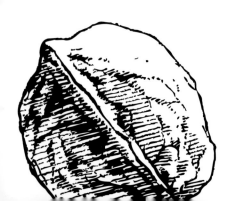

sun-dried tomato pesto

PREP TIME: 0:30

ingredients | Total Cost $5

2 cups sun-dried tomatoes (not the kind packed in oil) | $2

Juice and zest of one lemon | $0.50

3 cloves garlic, chopped | Pantry

2 tablespoons pine nuts | $2.50

1 teaspoon balsamic vinegar | Pantry

handful of fresh basil leaves | Pantry

1/2 cup extra-virgin olive oil | Pantry

salt and black pepper to taste | Pantry

directions | Makes about 1 cup of pesto

1. Soak the sun-dried tomatoes in hot water for 20-25 minutes before using, until plump.

2. Chop the sun-dried tomatoes roughly and combine with all ingredients except oil, salt, and pepper in the food processor. Run machine until ingredients have been very finely chopped. Drizzle in the olive oil and continue pulsing until a paste forms. Season with salt and pepper to taste.

chapter

3

firsts and sides

When I was a kid (and, um, still . . .), the whole point of Thanksgiving dinner was appetizers and sides. I lived for the cream cheese and red pepper jelly crackers my mom would assemble, the baked brie with apricot jam and the sweet potatoes, green beans, and stuffing served alongside the way-less-appealing 22-pound salt-and-herb-brined turkey. At restaurants, I often make a meal of a couple of appetizers or an appetizer and a salad, finding they are typically much more interesting than the entrees listed. Many of these make a quick meal on their own. I love packing the veggie spring rolls with a little container of peanut sauce as a take-along lunch and the rosemary sweet potatoes with goat cheese have made for a cheap and easy dinner at my house many a night.

WARNING:
BRINGING HOMEMADE
SPRING ROLLS TO A PARTY
DRAMATICALLY INCREASES
THE LIKELIHOOD THAT
SOMEONE WILL ASK FOR
YOUR PHONE NUMBER.

vegetarian vietnamese spring rolls

Whenever I bring these refreshing spring rolls to a party, I am inevitably the most popular girl there. People ooh and ahh over this complex-tasting and fancy-looking appetizer. Little do they know that it actually took me 20 minutes to pull together and cost me about seven bucks.

One note—when you are first learning to make these, I highly suggest buying extra ingredients and practicing on a batch before you make the ones you are going to serve guests. The delicate spring roll wrappers can break easily and assembling them can be somewhat difficult at first. But don't worry—even broken spring rolls are delicious!

PREP TIME 0:20

ingredients | Total Cost $7

10 rice paper spring roll wrappers | $1.50 for 30

20 fresh mint leaves | $1 for a bunch

1 red bell pepper, seeded and cut into matchsticks | $1.50

2 carrots shredded | $1

½ cucumber, peeled, seeded, and cut into matchsticks | $1

2 scallions (green onions) cut into thin 2-inch strips | $1 for a bunch

directions | Makes 10 spring rolls

1. Wet a wrapper under the tap or in a bowl of lukewarm water and shake gently to remove excess liquid. Lay wrapper on a clean, dry surface. Arrange a few pieces of mint in the center of the wrapper. Lay 2-3 pieces of bell pepper, a generous pinch of shredded carrots, a few pieces of cucumber and 1-2 slices of scallions on top of the mint, making sure that all ingredients are facing in the same direction. Once the wrapper is pliable enough to work with, tuck in the ends and roll up tightly, like a little burrito (don't worry if you mess a few up, this takes practice). Repeat until all ingredients are used up.

2. Serve sliced on the bias with peanut sauce (page 19), sweet chili sauce, or soy sauce.

green onion naan with yogurt-mint chutney

There's a great restaurant in San Francisco, called Dosa, which specializes in Indian breads. They serve a similar combination there and after dropping way too much money on it, having it several times one week, I decided to make it myself.

PREP TIME 0:50 | COOK TIME 0:10

ingredients | Total Cost $11

1 packet dry active dry yeast | $1.50 for 3

sugar or honey | Pantry

2 cups all-purpose flour, plus more for rolling | Pantry

1 teaspoon salt | Pantry

4 tablespoons melted butter, plus more for brushing | $1 for a stick

vegetable or canola oil | Pantry

2 large handfuls fresh mint leaves | $1 for a bunch

$\frac{1}{8}$ cup dried, unsweetened coconut | $1.50

Asian chili sauce to taste | $1.50 for 8 ounces

1 clove garlic, smashed | Pantry

1 small (1 inch) piece ginger, peeled and chopped | $0.50

$\frac{1}{4}$ cup plain yogurt | $1.50 for 8 ounces

$\frac{1}{2}$ teaspoon ground cumin | $1.50 for 1 ounce

couple dashes soy sauce | Pantry

4 scallions, chopped | $1 for a bunch

34

directions | Serves 3–6 (Makes 6 naans and about ½ cup chutney)

1. Combine ¾ cup warm water with the 1 teaspoon yeast and sugar until the yeast is dissolved. Cover and let stand in a warm place for 5 minutes, or until frothy.

2. Stir together the yeast and a salt in a large bowl add the yeast mixture and the butter. Mix into a soft dough then knead on a floured surface for about 5 minutes or until dough is smooth and elastic. Transfer to a lightly oiled bowl and cover with a clean kitchen towel or plastic wrap and let rise in a warm place for about 30 minutes or until the dough has doubled in size.

3. While dough rises, combine 2 teaspoons sugar or honey with all of the remaining ingredients except for the scallions in a food processor or blender and pulse until you have a thick chutney. Set aside until ready to use.

4. Punch down dough then knead for 5 minutes. Divide dough into six pieces. Sprinkle the scallions over the balls of dough and, using a rolling pin, roll each round out into an 8-inch circle or oblong shape.

5. Heat 1 tablespoon oil in a large frying pan over medium-high heat and fry a dough round for 1-2 minutes on each side. It should be browned in spots and become slightly puffy. Transfer to a clean plate (or baking sheet in a 200°F oven to keep the naan warm until serving time).

6. Continue frying the naans, adding more oil to the pan if necessary. Serve naan warm with the chutney for dipping.

sweet potato fries with sriracha aioli

Easy, delicious, and even relatively healthy. The Sriracha aioli is my secret ingredient: nothing more to it than spicy chili sauce and regular old mayonnaise, but it tastes so much more special.

PREP TIME 0:05 | COOK TIME 0:20

ingredients | Total Cost $3.75

1 large yam or 2 medium garnet yams (sweet potatoes), scrubbed and cut into 3 x ½-inch sticks | $1

1 tablespoon olive oil | Pantry

1 small bunch flat-leaf parsley, chopped | $0.75

4 tablespoons mayonnaise | Pantry

1-2 teaspoons Sriracha or other hot sauce | $2 for 10 ounces

salt and pepper to taste | Pantry

directions | Serves 2

1. Preheat oven to 425°F.

2. Spread yams on a baking sheet. Drizzle with the olive oil. Bake for 15-20 minutes or until crisp out the outside and tender inside. Toss with salt, pepper and parsley.

3. To make the aioli, simply stir Sriracha or other chili sauce into mayonnaise and serve alongside the fries.

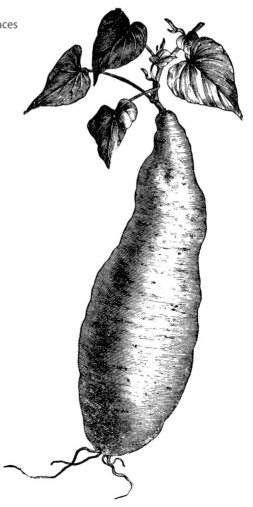

mashed sweet potatoes with goat cheese, rosemary, and olive oil

Will you still like me if I tell you mashed potatoes don't do all that much for me? I find them starchy and boring and just kind of . . . meh.

But this dish—this is something different altogether. This is my kind of root vegetable-based side dish. It's perfect alongside roasted meats, though it's not difficult for me to imagine eating a nice bowl of it with a crunchy salad for dinner.

PREP TIME: 0:10 | COOK TIME: 0:15

ingredients | Total Cost $6.50

4 medium or 3 large Garnet yams (sweet potatoes), peeled and cut into a large dice | $2

extra-virgin olive oil | Pantry

5 cloves of garlic, chopped | Pantry

1 sprig fresh rosemary leaves, chopped | $1 for a bunch

salt and pepper to taste | Pantry

2 ounces soft goat cheese | $3.50 for 4 ounces

directions | Serves 4

1. Bring a large pot of salted water to a boil over high heat. Add sweet potatoes and cook for 10-12 minutes, or until very soft.

2. While sweet potatoes cook, heat 3 tablespoons olive oil in a medium frying pan over low heat. Add the garlic and rosemary and cook for 8-10 minutes, stirring occasionally, until very fragrant (be very careful not to burn the garlic). Turn off heat.

3. Once the sweet potatoes have finished cooking, drain them and transfer to a mixing bowl. Smash, using the back of a fork or a potato masher.

4. Use a spatula to scrape the olive oil, garlic, and rosemary from the pan into the bowl. Stir well. Season with salt and pepper to taste.

5. Gently stir in the crumbled goat cheese (be careful not to stir too much—you want there to be little clumps and streaks of goat cheese).

6. Serve immediately, drizzled with a little more olive oil if desired.

ginger-shrimp potstickers with chili-scallion dipping sauce

The key with these is to use just a few simple, fresh ingredients so that the flavors really burst when you bite into them. They're also fantastic for entertaining because people are always impressed by how elegant they look and how delicious they taste . . . I think people imagine potstickers to be some sort of mystical, magical, unattainable entity—the unicorn of Chinese cooking. If only they knew that little more is needed to make fresh potstickers than simple ingredients, a frying pan with a fitted lid, and minimal small-motor skills . . .

*Note: If you keep Kosher, use chicken instead of the shrimp. Vegetarian? Use crumbled tofu or extra vegetables.

PREP TIME: 0:30 | COOK TIME: 0:08

ingredients | Total Cost $16.75

2 tablespoons vegetable oil, divided | Pantry

3 cloves garlic, minced | Pantry

1 small 2-inch piece of ginger, peeled and minced | $1

1/4 pound medium-sized raw shrimp, shelled, deveined, and chopped | $4

1 carrot, shredded | $0.50

1/2 red bell pepper, finely chopped | $1

1/3 cup frozen green peas | $1.50

6 tablespoons soy sauce, divided | $1.50 for 12 ounces

1 package (12-ounces) potsticker wrappers | $2

2 tablespoons rice vinegar | $2 for 12 ounces

Asian chili sauce to taste | $2.50 for 12 ounces

2 scallions, sliced | $0.75

directions | Makes about 30 potstickers

1. Heat the oil over medium-high heat in a large frying pan (be sure it has a fitted lid). Add the garlic and ginger and cook, stirring frequently for about a minute. Add the shrimp, carrot, bell pepper, and green peas and cook for another 2-3 minutes or until the shrimp become firm. Halfway through cooking, pour 2 tablespoons of the soy sauce over the shrimp-veggie mixture and stir well. When the shrimp have finished cooking, remove from heat and pour contents into a large bowl. Clean any leftover debris from pan and return to the stove for later use.

2. To assemble the potstickers, lay one potsticker wrapper on a clean, flat surface and put about 1 1/2 tablespoons of the filling in the center. Dip a clean finger or pastry brush into a small bowl of water and gently wet the edges. Gently pinch the corners together to form a point and seal the edges to seal in the filling. Set the assembled potstickers on a clean plate.

3. To cook, heat the remaining oil in the previously used frying pan over medium-high heat. Place as many potstickers as will fit into the pan and cook for 2-3 minutes, allowing the potstickers to develop a crisp crust on the bottom. Once crust has formed, pour 3 tablespoons water over the potstickers and immediately cover with the fitted lid. Allow to steam, covered for 2 minutes.

4. Carefully remove the lid and allow any excess water to cook away.

5. To make the sauce, combine the remaining soy sauce, rice vinegar, chili sauce to taste, and scallions and pour into little dipping bowls.

6. To serve, arrange on a plate with a little dipping bowl of the sauce.

henry's cheesy pepper biscuits

Henry, who is nine years old, is one of my favorite people to cook with, mostly because he (unlike many adults) likes to creatively personalize dishes and cook boldly, without fear of failing. Once, we made chicken soup together and, at the last minute, Henry suggested we also make biscuits. As I was stirring the dough, he suggested we add cheese and freshly ground black pepper to the dough. The results were delicious—flakey biscuits with gooey, salty bits of cheese and a peppery bite. Henry would also like you to know that, if you wanted to, you could add cut-up green onions to these (Henry loves green onions).

PREP TIME 0:10 | COOK TIME 0:16

ingredients | Total Cost $6.50

2 cups all-purpose flour, plus more for dusting and rolling | Pantry

4 teaspoons baking powder | Pantry

$^3/_4$ teaspoon salt, plus more for sprinkling | Pantry

1$^1/_2$ teaspoons freshly ground black pepper | Pantry

4 tablespoons very cold butter, cut into cubes | $1 for a stick

$^1/_2$ cup shredded sharp cheddar cheese, plus a few extra pinches for sprinkling | $3.50 for 12 ounces

1 cup buttermilk | $2 for a quart

directions | Makes about 12 biscuits

1. Preheat oven to 450°F. Lightly flour a baking sheet and set aside.

2. In a mixing bowl, combine the flour, baking powder, salt, and pepper.

3. Use your hands to rub the butter into the flour, until the mixture resembles small peas. Stir in the cheese.

4. Form a little well in the center of the mixture and pour in the buttermilk. Stir together to form a very sticky dough.

5. Lightly flour a flat, clean surface and knead the dough about five times, just until it holds together. Press it until it is about 1$^1/_2$ inches thick. Use a biscuit cutter, wine glass, or drinking glass to cut 3-inch circles out of the dough, reworking the scraps until all the dough has been cut.

6. Arrange the biscuits on the floured baking sheet so they touch one another lightly. Top each with a sprinkle of salt and a pinch of cheese.

7. Bake for 13-16 minutes, until puffy and golden-brown.

8. Serve hot.

cumin-laced black bean corn cakes

These savory cakes are sophisticated yet down-to-earth. If you want to serve them as appetizers, scale them down to 2-inch cakes and serve the sour cream on the side for dipping instead of as a garnish.

PREP TIME 0:20 | COOK TIME 0:10

ingredients | Total Cost $14

¹/₂ **cup cornmeal** | $2

³/₄ **cup flour** | Pantry

1 teaspoon baking powder | Pantry

¹/₂ **teaspoon baking soda** | Pantry

¹/₂ **teaspoon ground cumin** | $1.50 for 1 ounce

salt | Pantry

²/₃ **cup frozen white corn kernels** | $2 for 10 ounces

³/₄ **cup canned black beans, rinsed and drained** | $1 for 15 ounces

1 small bunch cilantro, chopped, divided | $1

1 cup milk | $1.50 for a pint

2 tablespoons vegetable oil, divided | Pantry

¹/₂ **teaspoon chili powder plus more for garnish** | $1.50 for 1 ounce

sour cream for garnish | $1.50 for 8 ounces

directions | Serves 2–3

1. Combine cornmeal, flour, baking powder, baking soda, ½ teaspoon. salt, and cumin. Stir until fully incorporated.

2. Whisk dry ingredients together with corn kernels, beans, cilantro, milk, and 1 tablespoon vegetable oil until a thick batter forms.

3. Heat remaining vegetable oil in a large frying pan over high heat. Drop batter in 3-tablespoon increments to form cakes that resemble breakfast pancakes, a few at a time, making sure not to crowd the pan.

4. Cook for 1-2 minutes on each side or until the sides dry and bubbles form on the tops. Flip and cook for another 1-2 minutes.

5. Arrange cakes on a plate. Combine avocado, onion, garlic, chili powder, and salt to taste to make guacamole. Serve cakes garnished with sour cream and a sprinkling of chili powder.

garlicky white bean dip

This easy dip is hummus' Italian first cousin. Perfect with fresh vegetables and baguette slices or spread on a sandwich, this delectable spread can be thrown together in just 5 minutes for a mere three dollars—and odds are good that you already have all the necessary ingredients on hand.

PREP TIME: 0:05

ingredients | Total Cost $3

1 can (15-ounces) white beans, such as Great Northern beans, drained and rinsed | $1.50

2 cloves garlic, peeled and smashed | Pantry

3 tablespoons extra-virgin olive oil, plus more for drizzling | Pantry

1 small bunch flat-leaf parsley plus more for garnish | $1

juice of ¹/₂ lemon | $0.50

salt and pepper to taste | Pantry

directions | Makes about 1½ cups dip.

1. Combine all ingredients in a food processor or blender until smooth and creamy. Serve garnished with more parsley and a drizzle of extra-virgin olive oil.

brown sugar-sriracha hot wings

These lip-smackingly delicious wings are smothered in a sweet-hot sauce, not for timid tongues. To cool them down, I recommend whirling together $^1/_3$ cup mayo, $^1/_3$ cup sour cream or yogurt and some finely chopped garlic and cilantro.

Note: This recipe makes about sixteen addictively good party wings, so if you are expecting a big crowd (or have friends with big appetites), you might consider doubling or tripling the recipe.

PREP TIME 0:45 | COOK TIME 0:25

ingredients | Total Cost $8.50

$^1/_8$ cup extra virgin olive oil plus more for the pan | Pantry

$^1/_2$ cup (packed) brown sugar | Pantry

$^1/_3$ cup soy sauce | Pantry

$^1/_8$ cup Sriracha | $2 for 17 ounces

4 cloves garlic, smashed | Pantry

1 $^1/_2$ pounds chicken "party wings" | $6.50

directions | Makes about sixteen wings (serves 2–4, depending on appetites)

1. Preheat oven to 400°F. Lightly oil a baking sheet.

2. Whisk together the olive oil, brown sugar, soy sauce, Sriracha, and smashed garlic. Transfer to an airtight container with a fitted lid (a gallon-size zip-top plastic bag will work in the absence of a container). Add the party wings and toss well to coat. Refrigerate for at least 30 minutes (or as long as overnight).

3. Spread marinated wings in an even layer over the prepared baking sheet, reserving remaining marinade. Bake wings for 15 minutes, then flip and cook for another 7-8 minutes, or until chicken is cooked through but still tender.

4. While chicken bakes, transfer remaining marinade to a small pot and bring to a boil over medium-high heat (to kill bacteria). Reduce to medium low and simmer for 4-5 minutes, or until the marinade becomes very thick and syrupy.

5. Just before serving, brush the chicken wings with a coat or two of the reduced marinade.

college nachos

Back in college, my friends and I would stumble back to my Allston, MA apartment at 3 A.M., after the usual libations (mostly "jungle juice" and Jell-O shots) to hang out. I would shuffle off to the kitchen and open the fridge to see what we had, which, frequently, wasn't much. Somehow though, I almost always could find the makings for nachos, which were then immediately consumed with gusto by my friends.

Since then, I've dropped many of my college habits (ahem—Crystal Light and bottom-shelf vodka . . .), but these nachos are the real deal. No Velveeta American cheese nonsense. Just real ingredients baked onto chips, topped with more fresh, real ingredients. So good, sober grown-ups love them too.

Note: If you don't have chips but you do have tortillas (any kind will do), cut them into wedges, toss lightly with vegetable or canola oil and a little salt, and bake at 375°F for 15 minutes until crisp.

PREP TIME 0:20 | COOK TIME 0:12

ingredients | Total Cost $12

6 cups tortilla chips | $2 for 16 ounces

½ (15-ounces) can black beans, rinsed and drained | $1.50

1 cup shredded mozzarella, cheddar, or jack cheese | $3 for 8 ounces

1 green jalapeño pepper, seeded and sliced (leave the seeds intact if you really like spice) | $0.50

1 avocado, diced | $1.50

3 tablespoon sour cream or Mexican crema | $1.50 for 15 ounces

1 small bunch cilantro, chopped | $1

½ red onion, diced | $0.50

1 Roma tomato, cored and diced | $0.50

directions | Serves 4–6

1. Preheat oven to 375°F.

2. Spread chips over an ungreased baking sheet. Scatter beans over the chips. Cover with shredded cheese and bake for 10-12 minutes, or until cheese is melted and bubbly.

3. Top baked nachos with jalapeño, avocado, sour cream or crema, cilantro, onion, and tomato.

4. Serve immediately.

ONLY MAKE THESE NACHOS IF YOU LIKE GOOEY, MELTED CHEESE, FRESH GUACAMOLE AND HAVING YOUR PRAISES SUNG LOUDLY.

pepperoni pizza spirals

I love Stromboli (an Italian turnover stuffed with pizza ingredients) and wanted to make some for a cocktail party I was throwing, but hated the idea of my guests having to hover over plates to catch the cheesy, goopy fillings as they ate them, so I decided to roll and cut my Stromboli like cinnamon rolls. The result? A perfectly neat, hand-holdable, delicious spiral of pizza. Yum.

PREP TIME 0:20 | COOK TIME 0:15

ingredients | Total Cost $11

flour for rolling and for dusting pan | Pantry

1 recipe pizza dough | $1.50

³/₄ cup tomato sauce | $1.50 for a 15-ounces can

1¹/₂ cups shredded provolone or mounceszarella cheese | $3.50 for 8 ounces

about 12 slices pepperoni, chopped | $3.50 for 6 ounces

1 handful fresh basil leaves, chopped | $1 for a bunch

directions | Makes about 10 spirals (serves 4–6)

1. Preheat oven to 400°F. Lightly flour a baking sheet and set aside.

2. Place pizza dough onto a lightly floured surface and use a rolling pin to roll it out into an approximately 18 x 14-inch rectangle.

3. Spread tomato sauce over the entire top surface of the dough. Sprinkle the cheese evenly over the sauce. Top cheese with pepperoni and chopped basil.

4. Starting at the bottom and pinching as you go, roll the dough up tightly, so you have a 14-inch cylinder.

5. Use a sharp knife to slice cylinder into about ten even rolls. Place rolls, spiral-side-up, on the prepared baking sheet.

6. Bake 12-15 minutes, or until rolls are golden-brown and cheese is bubbly.

7. Cool 5 minutes, then serve warm.

crostini 3 ways

Crostini are the number-one way to convince guests that you are a detail-oriented gour-met chef, while actually being lazy and cheap. All you really need is bread, a spreadable cheese (though I would recommend against Cheez-Whiz . . .) and a topping.

PREP TIME 0:20 | COOK TIME 0:30

ingredients | Total Cost $7.25

extra-virgin olive oil | Pantry

1 onion, sliced thin | $0.50

1 tablespoon balsamic vinegar | Pantry

1 baguette, sliced into ½"-thick slices | $1.50

6 ounces ricotta or cream cheese | $3 for 14 ounces

1 jalapeño, sliced very thin | $0.25

honey | Pantry

your favorite fruit preserves | $2 for 12 ounces

black pepper to taste | Pantry

directions | Serves 4–6

1. Preheat oven to 375°F.

2. Drizzle 3 tablespoon olive oil into a medium frying pan over medium-low heat. Add onion and cook for 18-20 minutes, stirring occasionally, until caramelized. Drizzle with balsamic vinegar and cook for 2-3 more minutes. Remove from heat.

3. Arrange baguette slices on a baking sheet and drizzle lightly with olive oil. Bake for 8-10 minutes or until lightly crisp. Let cool.

4. Spread baguette slices liberally with ricotta or cream cheese.

5. Top ⅓ of the slices with 2-3 slices jalapeño and a drizzle of honey.

6. Top ⅓ of the slices with a few pinches of caramelized onions.

7. Top ⅓ of the slices with a spoonful of preserves.

8. Top all crostini with a sprinkle of freshly-ground black pepper.

broccoli-kale gratin

If you or someone you love (hi, Dad!) has not yet learned to appreciate kale and/or broccoli steamed or sautéed lightly, topped with little more than a squeeze of lemon juice and some salt and pepper, this recipe is for you. It's essentially a classier version of broccoli with cheese sauce.

Or, if you, like me, already appreciate simply-prepared broccoli and/or kale and just really like decadent, mac-and-cheese-esque preparations of vegetables, this dish is also for you.

It's substantial enough to serve as a vegetarian entree, but would also be good served, in smaller quantities, alongside grilled meat.

PREP TIME 0:20 | COOK TIME: 0:35

ingredients | Total Cost $12

2 medium heads broccoli, florets and stem chopped | $1

3 cups kale leaves, chopped (about ¹/₃ bunch Tuscan kale or 4 leaves Dino kale) | $1 for a bunch

1 tablespoon olive oil | Pantry

2 cloves garlic, chopped | Pantry

¹/₂ medium onion, chopped | $0.50 for a whole onion

2 cups heavy cream | $2.50 for a pint

few pinches nutmeg | $1.50 for 1 ounce

³/₄ cup sharp white cheddar cheese, shredded, plus more for topping | $3.50 for 8 ounces

salt and pepper to taste | Pantry

¹/₂ cup raw almonds, chopped/crushed | $2 (buy in the bulk section)

directions | Serves 4

1. Preheat the oven to 400°F.

2. Bring a large pot of lightly salted water to a boil and add the kale and broccoli. Cook for 4-5 minutes, so they're tender-crisp and retain their green color. Drain and rinse under cool water. Set aside.

3. Heat the olive oil in a medium pot over medium heat. Add the garlic and onion and cook for 3-4 minutes, until very fragrant. Stir in the cream and nutmeg and continue to cook, stirring occasionally, until slightly thickened, 3-4 minutes. Add the cheese, stir to melt, and season with salt and pepper to taste. Remove from heat.

4. Stir the cooked broccoli and kale into the cream sauce and combine well. Divide between four ramekins or oven-proof bowls. Top each with a few pinches of cheese and a sprinkle of the almonds.

5. Bake for 22-25 minutes, until golden-brown and bubbly. If desired, place under a broiler set to high for 1-2 minutes to create more of a crusted top.

6. Let cool slightly, then serve.

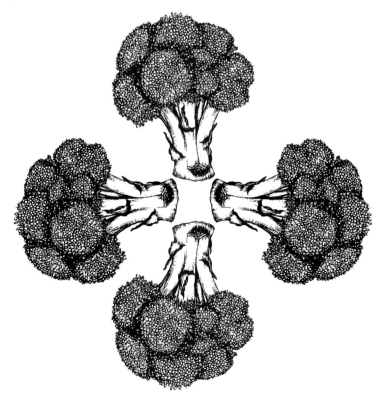

sriracha-glazed carrots

When we were little, my brother and I had distinctly different eating styles. While an early-in-life petting zoo incident led me to stay away from anything that ever had a face (a phase which lasted nearly twenty years), he refused to eat anything that ever had a root. My parents, of course, insisted he eat some kind of vegetable and so every night they would put three baby carrots on his plate along with whatever protein and starch they were serving, and every night he would pretend to choke them down while actually stuffing them in his pockets. Inevitably, he would forget they were there and toss his pants in the family hamper at the end of the night. On laundry day, my mom would discover a dozen petrified baby carrots at the bottom of the dryer. Now that he's older, however, his palate has developed and he actually clamors for this spicy-sweet rendition of his former mortal-enemy-in-the-form-of-a-vegetable. Slow-roasting draws the carrots' natural sugars out, while a slightly sweet and spicy glaze makes them more special than simple buttered carrots. I like to serve these alongside grilled meats.

PREP TIME 0:05 | COOK TIME 0:20

ingredients | Total Cost $6

2 pounds peeled baby carrots (I prefer to use actual baby carrots, known as petites carrottes, with the tips of their stems intact) | $3

extra-virgin olive oil | Pantry

salt and pepper to taste | Pantry

1 tablespoon unsalted butter, melted | $1 for a stick

Sriracha to taste (I usually use about 2 teaspoons) | $2 for 16 ounces

1 tablespoon honey | Pantry

directions | Serves 3–4

1. Preheat oven to 375°F.
2. Spread carrots out on a baking sheet and drizzle with olive oil. Use your hands to toss the carrots, ensuring they are well-coated. Season with salt and pepper to taste.
3. Roast for 18-20 minutes, rotating halfway through.
4. In a small bowl toss together the butter, Sriracha, and honey.
5. Drizzle over cooked carrots and toss to coat. Serve warm.

chapter

4

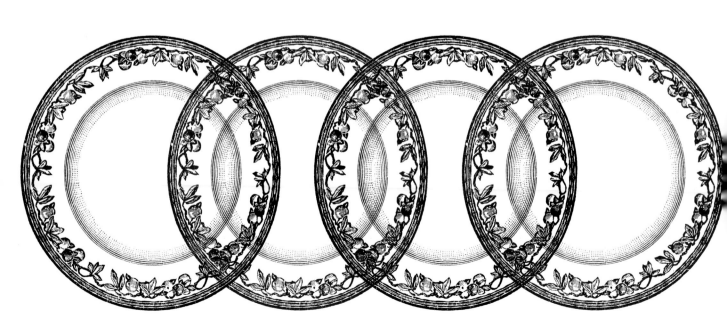

taking stock

Soup is perhaps one of the most economical ways to satisfy both appetites and palates—and I'm not talking about opening up a can of Campbell's. A bubbling pot of soup or stew needs little help to become a complete meal. Maybe some crusty bread or a biscuit or two. Perhaps a little salad. But even if you skip these amenities, you'll still be able to fill tummies and keep the occupants of your dinner table satisfied and happy.

Another great money-saving trick when it comes to soups and stews, which you'll see me suggest throughout this chapter, is to make a big pot on a Sunday evening and fill individual-serving-sized airtight containers with it. Then refrigerate (or even freeze) and throughout the week, simply microwave a container (with the lid removed) for hot, healthy, and delicious lunches or dinners whenever you want them.

spicy black bean soup

This simple soup has all of the bean-y, spicy, onion-y flavors of a hearty vegetarian chili, but the smooth, elegant presentation of a puree soup. This is a great recipe to use an immersion blender for (though a food processor or blender will do just fine).

PREP TIME 0:10 | COOK TIME 0:15

ingredients | Total Cost $7

Extra-Virgin olive oil | Pantry

1 small white onion, chopped | $0.50

2 cloves garlic, minced | Pantry

2 (15-ounce) cans black beans, drained and rinsed | $3

1/2 tsp cumin | $1.50 for 1 oz.

1 small jalapeño, seeded and chopped | $0.25

1 handful cilantro leaves, chopped, stems reserved and cleaned | $1

salt and pepper to taste | Pantry

1 Roma tomato, seeded and chopped | $0.50

directions | Serves 3–4

1. In a large saucepan, heat 1 tablespoon olive oil over medium heat. Add onion and cook for 2-3 minutes, until soft. Add garlic, stir, and allow to cook for another minute.

2. Add beans, cumin, jalapeño, cilantro stems, and 1 cup of water. Stir to combine and cook for 10 minutes uncovered. Puree until smooth using either an immersion blender, a food processor, or a regular blender. Add salt and pepper to taste and thin out using a little water if necessary.

3. Serve, in bowls, garnished with the chopped cilantro and tomato.

spicy corn chowder

Humble corn chowder seems to me to be something of a long-forgotten underdog soup. This lovely rendition features the bright flavors of chili powder and fresh scallions as well as the traditional corn, potatoes, and onions. I highly recommend serving it with toasted baguette slices as fresh croutons.

PREP TIME 0:15 | COOK TIME 0:20

ingredients | Total Cost $11

$1/2$ **white onion, diced** | $0.50

1 medium baking potato, scrubbed and diced | $0.50

4 scallions, sliced | $1

1 cup fresh or frozen corn kernels | $2

2 tablespoons unsalted butter | $1 for a stick

4 tablespoons flour | Pantry

$1/2$ **to 1 teaspoon chili powder** | $1.50 for 1 ounce

$1/2$ **teaspoon cumin** | $1.50 for 1 ounce

$1/2$ **cup half-and-half** | $1 for $1/2$ pint

salt and pepper to taste | Pantry

$1/4$ **cup grated jack (or pepper jack) cheese** | $2

directions | Serves 2–3

1. Melt the butter in a soup pot over medium heat. Sprinkle in the flour and whisk together until a thick paste forms. Slowly add 3 $1/2$ cups of water, whisking constantly until a milky broth develops. Add the onions and potatoes to the broth. Increase heat to high and cook for 10-12 minutes or until potatoes are cooked through.

2. Add the corn and most of the scallion slices (reserve a few pinches for garnish). Stir in the half-and-half and more water if necessary to bring the soup to a creamy, chowderlike consistency. Add chili powder, cumin, salt, and pepper. Adjust seasonings as necessary. Stir in cheese until melted and fully incorporated.

3. To serve, ladle into bowls and garnish with scallions and croutons if desired.

chicken soup with dumplings

This homey, soothing full-meal soup is my mom's recipe. She would make large batches of it and serve it over the course of a couple of days. You can use dried herbs here, but fresh ones really kick it up several notches.

PREP TIME 0:30 | COOK TIME 2:00

ingredients | Total Cost $16

About 6 chicken legs, skin intact | $4

1 onion, chopped | $0.50

2 ribs of celery , sliced | $0.50

1 clove garlic, minced | Pantry

2 carrots sliced into coins | $0.50

1 teaspoon fresh thyme leaves | $1 for a bunch

2 bay leaves | $1 for a bunch

1 small bunch parsley, minced and divided in half | $1 for a bunch

15-20 whole peppercorns | Pantry

12 cups water

1 (15-ounce) can low-sodium chicken broth | $1.50

1 cup sifted flour | Pantry

1 teaspoon baking powder | Pantry

$\frac{1}{2}$ teaspoon salt | Pantry

1 tablespoon butter | $1 for a stick

2 tablespoons fresh rosemary chopped | $1 for a bunch

1 teaspoon fresh dill, chopped | $1 for a bunch

1 egg | $1.50 for 12

3 tablespoons milk | $1.50 for a pint

directions | Serves 4 generously with leftovers

1. Rinse chicken legs and pat dry with paper towels. Place onion, celery, garlic, and carrots in the bottom of a large soup pot. Add thyme, bay leaves, half of the parsley, and peppercorns. Place chicken on top of vegetables and spices and add water and low sodium chicken broth. Bring to a boil, turn down to a simmer and cook for 1 $\frac{1}{2}$ hours. Remove chicken and let cool. When cool, remove skin and bones, shred chicken meat, and return to pot.

2. Prepare dumpling batter: Combine flour, baking powder, and salt. Cut shortening/butter into flour mixture and add rosemary, dill, and the remaining parsley. In a separate bowl, whisk together egg and milk; add to dry mixture and stir with fork until well blended. Bring chicken soup to a very low boil and drop dumplings by teaspoonfuls into chicken soup. Turn soup down to a simmer and cover and steam for 10 minutes, and then simmer 10 minutes more with lid off until dumplings are fluffy and done inside. Leftovers are awesome the next day.

THIS ONION SOUP WILL PUT

A SPRING IN YOUR STEP.

(SORRY IF THAT WAS TOO CORNY).

white corn and spring onion soup

I first had this soup with my friend Doug, one particularly wonderful evening when he visited San Francisco and took me to an adorable downtown French bistro, Café Claude. This white corn-spring onion puree soup absolutely blew me away. The best thing about it was that I could so cleanly taste all of the flavors: fresh corn, onion, and cream. Though Café Claude was decidedly not BrokeAss, my version of this soup is cheap and easy to make. Best of all, it tastes like summer in a bowl.

PREP TIME 0:10 | COOK TIME 0:20

ingredients | Total Cost $5.50

1 tablespoon extra-virgin olive oil | Pantry

1¹/₂ cups frozen (or fresh) white corn kernels | $1.50 for a 10-ounce bag

3 spring onions, sliced, ends removed | $1

1 can vegetable broth | $1 15 ounces

1 medium Russet potato, peeled and diced | $0.50

1 cup 2-percent milk | $1.50 for a pint

salt and pepper to taste | Pantry

¹/₂ small baguette, sliced | $1

1 clove garlic, cut in half | Pantry

directions | Serves 2

1. Heat olive oil in a soup pot over medium-high heat. Add spring onions and sauté for 2-3 minutes or until slightly soft. Add corn, potatoes, and vegetable broth. Cover and cook for 10-12 minutes or until potatoes are soft.

2. Use an immersion blender to puree directly in the pot or transfer to a food processor or blender. Puree until smooth and return to the pot.

3. Whisk in the milk and cook over medium-high heat for 5-6 minutes, stirring frequently. Season well with salt and pepper.

4. While the soup cooks, toast the baguette slices, either in the toaster or in a 450°F oven. Lightly rub the toasted slices with the garlic. Serve the soup with garlic croutons as a garnish.

sweet potato, chicken, and white bean stew

This easy, hearty stew is full of healthy fiber (thanks to the beans) and lean protein (courtesy of the chicken and the beans again), and is spiked with the sweet heat of chili powder and cumin. Top with the listed garnishes if you so desire and feel free to add shredded cheese, sour cream, or fresh salsa.

Also, should a cup of this chili-esque stew happen to be poured over some tortilla chips and then topped with shredded cheddar cheese, popped under the broiler, and then topped with more onions, cilantro, and avocado, it would not be the worst thing ever to happen. Just so you know.

PREP TIME 0:15 | COOK TIME 0:25

ingredients | Total Cost $10

1 tablespoon extra-virgin olive oil | Pantry

1 medium onion, diced (reserve a few pinches for garnish) | $0.50

3 cloves garlic, chopped | Pantry

1 medium sweet potato (garnet yam), scrubbed and diced | $0.50

2 boneless, skinless chicken breasts, chopped into bite-size pieces | $5

2 (15-ounce) cans white (cannellini or Great Northern) beans, rinsed and drained | $2.50

1 teaspoon Ancho chili powder | $1.50 for 1 ounce

$\frac{1}{2}$ teaspoon ground cumin | $1.50 for 1 ounce

salt and pepper to taste | Pantry

directions | Serves 2–4

1. Heat olive oil in a large pot over medium heat. Add onion and cook for 2-3 minutes or until translucent. Add garlic, sweet potato, chicken, beans, cumin, and chili powder. Stir well and add water to cover (about 3 cups). Cover pot and cook for 18-20 minutes, or until sweet potato is soft and chicken has cooked through.

2. Serve, garnished with the reserved onion, plus cilantro and/or avocado if desired.

pea soup with scallions, basil, and parmesan

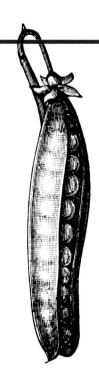

Fresh basil and peas are a brilliant combination, simultaneously perking one another up, while nutty Parmesan gives a depth of flavor that makes you remember this soup. Another plus? You basically just dump a bunch of stuff in a pot, cook it, and then puree. Plus, it's delicious served either hot or cold.

PREP TIME 0:05 | COOK TIME 0:15

ingredients | Total Cost $10

1 (10 ounce) bag frozen green peas | $1.50

1 (15 ounce) can chicken or vegetable stock | $1

6 scallions, chopped, ends removed, plus more for garnish | $1

2 tablespoons unsalted butter | $1.50 for a stick

1 small bunch basil, chopped | $1

2 tablespoons grated Parmesan, plus more for garnish | $4 for 12 ounces

salt and pepper to taste | Pantry

directions | Serves 2–4

1. Combine green peas, stock, scallions, butter, basil, and Parmesan in a soup pot over medium-high heat. Stir until the butter melts. Bring to a light boil and then reduce heat to medium. Allow to simmer for 10 minutes or until peas are soft.

2. Remove from heat and puree using a food processor, blender or immersion blender. Season with salt and pepper to taste.

3. If serving chilled, refrigerate for at least 2 hours or until cold. If serving hot, serve immediately, garnishing individual bowls with Parmesan and scallions.

white bean, leek, and bacon soup

This wildly inexpensive and simple soup is so deeply satisfying and luxurious-tasting that it can make a perfectly lovely meal on its own. If I'm having company over, I serve it with spinach-cranberry salad and crusty sourdough rolls.

PREP TIME 0:10 | COOK TIME 0:20

ingredients | Total Cost $6

2 (15-ounce) cans white beans | $3

1 small leek, ends removed and sliced (reserve a few thin slices for garnish) | $0.50

2 slices thick-cut bacon, chopped | $1

1/8 cup half-and-half | $1.50 for a pint

salt and pepper to taste | Pantry

directions | Serves 2–4

1. Combine beans, leek slices, bacon, and 2 cups water in a soup pot. Cover tightly and cook over medium-high heat for 15 minutes or until leeks are soft and fragrant. Puree using an immersion blender, regular blender, or food processor. Stir in half-and-half and salt and pepper to taste (make sure to taste it as the bacon provides a fair amount of salt).

2. Cook for another 5 minutes on medium-low heat, stirring frequently.

3. Serve garnished with leek slices.

pork pho

Pho is one of those foods that periodically inspires intense cravings for most people I know. Amazingly flavorful broth with soft-yet-chewy rice noodles, meat, and an array of add-ins that contribute an assortment of flavors and textures—you just can't beat it. And yet, I know few people who actually make it at home, which is strange because it's so easy and cheap. This recipe will easily feed 2-3 people for less than twelve dollars total. Make sure to buy your ingredients at an Asian specialty grocery store for the best prices and selection.

PREP TIME 0:30 | COOK TIME 1:15

ingredients | Total Cost $11.75

1 pound pork tenderloin, half chopped coarsely, half thinly sliced | $2

5 cloves garlic, finely minced | Pantry

1 small piece ginger, finely minced | $0.50

1 teaspoon ground star anise | $1.50 for 1 ounce

2 stalks lemongrass, chopped | $1

1 tablespoon brown sugar | Pantry

1 tablespoon salt | Pantry

freshly ground pepper | Pantry

1 bunch cilantro, stems removed and reserved | $1

1 red onion, half chopped coarsely, half thinly sliced | $0.50

1 pound rice vermicelli noodles | $1

1 lemon, cut into wedges | $0.50

1 green jalapeño, sliced into rings | $0.25

2 cups mung bean sprouts | $1

hoisin sauce | $2 for 8 ounces

Asian chili sauce or Sriracha | $2 for 12 ounces

directions | Serves 3–4

1. Fill a pot with 3 quarts water. Add coarsely chopped pork, garlic, ginger, star anise, lemongrass, brown sugar, salt, pepper, cilantro stems, and coarsely chopped onion. Cover, bring to a boil and then reduce to a simmer. Allow to simmer for 45 minutes and up to two hours. Strain broth, discard solids, and return broth to pot.

2. In a separate bowl, cook noodles according to package directions. Drain and rinse.

3. Bring broth to a boil and add thinly sliced pork. Cook until pork is no longer pink, about 10 minutes.

4. To serve, use a ladle to portion broth into bowls. Use tongs to add noodles and pork to bowls. Serve with cilantro leaves, sliced red onion, lemon wedges, jalapeño, bean sprouts, hoisin sauce and chili sauce or Sriracha to add in.

ridiculously easy turkey chili

Even if you think you can't cook, you can make this chili. Using prepared pico de gallo is a simple trick that gives the chili a boost in the flavor and texture departments and tastes fresher than canned tomatoes. It's easy, fast, cheap, and delicious. Make a big pot of this on a Sunday and eat it all week.

PREP TIME 0:10 | COOK TIME 0:20

ingredients | Total Cost $13

1 tablespoon extra virgin olive oil | Pantry

1 onion, chopped | $0.50

3 cloves garlic, minced | Pantry

1 pound lean ground turkey | $3

2 (15-ounce) cans black beans, drained | $3

1 (16-ounce) container pico de gallo (preferably the refrigerated kind) | $3.50

1 teaspoon cumin | $1.50 for 1 ounce

1 teaspoon chili powder | $1.50 for 1 ounce

salt and pepper to taste | Pantry

directions | Serves 4–6

1. Heat olive oil in a large pot over medium-high heat. Add onions and garlic and cook, stirring frequently, for 2-3 minutes, until fragrant. Add ground turkey and allow turkey to brown, stirring occasionally, 4-5 minutes.

2. Add beans, pico de gallo, cumin, chili powder, and salt and pepper to taste. Stir well and reduce heat to medium-low. Cook for 10-12 minutes until hot and bubbly. If chili becomes too thick while cooking, add a little water.

3. Serve hot, as is or garnished with shredded cheese, cilantro, chopped onions, sour cream, avocado, hot sauce, etc.

MAKE CHILI,

NOT EXCUSES.

watermelon-lime gazpacho

In addition to being yummy to eat and adorable to look at, the watermelon "bowls" don't need to be washed, which means fewer dishes which means more time to lounge outside, enjoying this yummy soup.

PREP TIME 0:20

ingredients | Total Cost $9.50

1 baby seedless watermelon | $3

1 cup tomato juice | $2 for 32 ounces

1 clove garlic | Pantry

1 handful fresh cilantro leaves, finely chopped | $1 for a bunch

$1/4$ red onion, very finely diced | $0.50 for a whole onion

$1/2$ cucumber, peeled, seeded, and finely chopped | $1.50 for a whole cucumber

$1/2$ red bell pepper, seeded and finely chopped | $1 for whole bell pepper

juice of 1 lime | $0.50

3 tablespoons extra-virgin olive oil | Pantry

1 tablespoon balsamic vinegar | Pantry

salt and pepper to taste | Pantry

directions | Serves 2

1. Cut the watermelon in half and slice a very thin piece of the rind off to make a flat bottom, being careful not to cut through to the flesh (so the watermelon half can be used as a bowl).

2. Use a spoon to scrape most of the watermelon flesh out of the rind and transfer it into a bowl. Take care not to make any holes in the bottom of the watermelon "bowl." Pick out any black seeds that you can, but don't worry too much about them.

3. Place watermelon flesh, tomato juice, garlic, cilantro, and half each of the onion, cucumber, and bell pepper in a blender or food processor. Add the lime juice, olive oil, balsamic vinegar, salt and pepper, and puree lightly (it should be mostly smooth with a few chunks). Transfer to a bowl (preferably a spouted one) or pitcher.

4. Stir in the remaining vegetables, stir well and adjust seasonings if necessary.

5. Pour into the watermelon "bowls" and serve, garnished with lime or cilantro, if desired.

fire-roasted tomato soup with grilled cheese bites

I'm normally somewhat hesitant to use canned fruits or vegetables, but I make one exception: Muir Glen Fire Roasted Tomatoes. They are organic, readily available, not too expensive, and absolutely delicious. The fire-roasting technique used on them imparts a sweet-yet-earthy flavor that gives serious depth to dishes with practically zero effort on the chef's part. This soup is so freaking easy and quick to throw together, giving you extra time to make equally simple-yet-glorious grilled cheese bites.

PREP TIME 0:10 | COOK TIME 0:25

ingredients | Total Cost $12

1 tablespoon extra-virgin olive oil | Pantry

4 cloves garlic, chopped | Pantry

1 medium onion, chopped | $0.50

2 (14.5-ounce) cans fire-roasted crushed tomatoes | $4.50

¼ cup half-and-half | Pantry

salt and pepper to taste | Pantry

4 slices sandwich bread | $2.50 for a loaf

2 slices cheese of your choice (I like pepper jack) | $3.50 for 8 ounces

2 tablespoons unsalted butter (at room temerature) | $1 for a stick

directions | Serves 3–4

1. Heat olive oil in a soup pot over medium heat. Add garlic and onions and cook, stirring occasionally, for 4–5 minutes, or until onions are translucent and very fragrant. Add tomatoes and cook, covered for 15 minutes. Stir occasionally.

2. While soup cooks, assemble the grilled cheese by sandwiching each slice of cheese between two pieces of bread. Spread the outsides of the sandwiches with the butter. Heat a frying pan over medium-high heat and grill the sandwiches until the cheese melts and the bread is golden-brown. Turn heat off and leave sandwiches in the warm pan until ready to serve.

3. Puree the soup using a blender, food processor, or immersion blender. Return to pot, stir in the half-and half, and season with salt and pepper to taste. Cook, uncovered, over medium heat for 5 minutes.

4. Cut the grilled cheeses into 1-inch squares, ladle the hot soup into bowls and serve.

rosemary-shallot beef stew

Beef stew is the ultimate "set it and forget it" on-a-budget dinner. With just a little mindful prep, cheap, tough, chewy chuck roast turns meltingly tender and flavorful as it stews at a low temperature for an hour-and-a-half. Many people like to add wine to their stew, but I find balsamic vinegar imparts a touch of wine flavor and much-needed acid for less money.

PREP TIME 0:25 | COOK TIME 1:45

ingredients | Total Cost $13.50

1 pound "stew beef," (also known as chuck roast or shoulder), cut into 1½" cubes | $6

2 tablespoon all-purpose flour | Pantry

extra-virgin olive oil | Pantry

3 large shallots, thinly sliced | $1

5 cloves garlic, smashed | Pantry

1 quart beef broth | $2.50

few sprigs fresh rosemary | $1 for a bunch

6 new (baby) potatoes, scrubbed and quartered (skin intact) | $2

3 carrots, peeled and cut lengthwise and then into thirds | $1

2 tablespoons balsamic vinegar | Pantry

salt and pepper to taste | Pantry

directions | Serves 4

1. Toss the beef cubes in the flour to lightly coat, shaking off excess.

2. Heat 2 tablespoons olive oil in a Dutch oven or other large soup pot over medium-high heat. Add beef and cook, undisturbed, for 2-3 minutes. Turn beef over and cook for another 2-3 minutes.

3. Reduce heat to medium, add 1 tablespoon olive oil to the pan and add the sliced shallots. Cook, stirring occasionally, for 3-4 minutes, or until shallots have softened and become very fragrant. Add the garlic and cook for another minute, stirring occasionally.

4. Deglaze the pan by adding ½ cup of the stock and scraping the browned bits at the bottom of the pan and stirring into the soup. Continue scraping (and adding more stock if necessary) until all browned bits have been scraped away. Add the rest of the stock, 1 cup of water, the rosemary, potatoes, carrots, and balsamic vinegar. Reduce heat to low.

5. Cover pot and cook for 1 hour and 30 minutes. After 1 hour, check the stew, and add a bit more water if necessary. The stew is done when the beef is tender enough to be easily pulled apart with a fork.

6. Ladle into bowls and serve.

chapter

5

between bread (and tortillas)

Whenever I tell people I write about food for a living, they typically ask me one of two questions: a) "What's your favorite thing to cook?" (Answer: it varies depending on the day, but typically anything involving peanut sauce is in the running), or b) "If you had to eat one thing for the rest of your life, what would it be?" To that, I always say "A vegetarian burrito with black beans, rice, guacamole, sour cream, salsa, onions, and cilantro." Why? Well, in addition to being a completely delicious (to me, anyway) and highly complete meal, featuring protein, fiber, vegetables, and calcium, it's portable (which would likely be convenient in the imaginary post-apocalyptic world in which I can only eat one thing for the rest of my life . . .). Portability is something I've come to really appreciate in food. I'm an avid hiker and picnicker, and consider the ideal sunny day spent in the woods, by a lake, or on the side of a mountain with a backpack full of tasty foods and maybe a bottle of wine. Sandwiches, tacos, and even quesadillas taste even better to me when the view is pretty and the sun is warming my shoulders.

Foods between slices of bread or tortillas make for a cheap and easy way to throw together lunch or dinner in any setting. Many of these also make great bring-along brown bag lunches for work or school .

beer-battered fish tacos

Take a trip down to San Diego, CA and you'll find these tacos everywhere. They are quintessential surfer fuel, but you can make them in the comfort of your own home. I can't tell you what to do, but I like to sip the rest of the beer straight out of the bottle while I make these.

PREP TIME 0:30 | COOK TIME 0:06

ingredients | Total Cost $16.50

½ cup (4 ounces) inexpensive pilsner | $5 for a six-pack

⅔ cup flour plus more for dusting fish | Pantry

salt | Pantry

½ pound red snapper or tilapia fillets (2-3 small fillets) | $3

vegetable oil for frying | Pantry

1 avocado, diced | $1.50

1 mango, diced | $1

½ red onion, diced | $0.50

juice of ½ lime | $0.50

½ jalapeño, seeded and finely diced | $0.50

1 small bunch cilantro, chopped | $1

2 Roma tomatoes, diced | $1

6 corn tortillas | $1.50 for thirty

directions | Makes 6 tacos

1. Combine beer, flour, and a pinch of salt in a bowl. Whisk until a smooth batter is achieved. Set aside.

2. Cut fish into 3-inch pieces, removing small bones if possible. Pour a little flour onto a plate. Lightly dredge fish pieces in flour, shaking off excess. Set aside.

3. Heat about 1" inch vegetable oil in a deep skillet over high heat. Move floured fish and batter near the stove. Dip the floured fish pieces into the batter, ensuring each piece is fully coated and excess drips off. Fry fish pieces, a few at a time, until golden brown and crisp on one side. Use metal tongs or a metal spatula to flip them and cook on the other side. Remove carefully and drain on paper towels.

4. Combine avocado, mango, onion, lime, jalapeño, cilantro, tomato, and a pinch of salt. Stir to combine.

5. To assemble tacos, top each corn tortilla with a few pieces of fish, and couple of large spoonfuls of salsa.

spinach-squash quesadillas

OK, I realize this is barely a recipe. It's really just a bunch of stuff thrown into a tortilla and pan-fried, but honestly, it's so yummy, easy, and even moderately healthy, that I just had to include it. These make for a perfect snack, lunch, or even a quick supper alongside a bowl of soup.

Note: If you have some cooked, smashed squash lying around, use that, but honestly, canned, unsweetened pumpkin is just perfect and super-easy.

PREP TIME 0:10 | COOK TIME 0:15

ingredients | Total Cost $11

2 tablespoons extra-virgin olive oil, divided | Pantry

1/2 red onion, sliced thin | $0.50

4 whole wheat burrito-size tortillas | $2.50 for twelve

1/2 cup peeled, cooked, smashed Winter squash (pumpkin, butternut, Acorn or Hubbard,) | $1.50

salt and pepper to taste | Pantry

1/2 cup shredded cheddar, mozzarella, or jack cheese | $3.50 for 8 ounces

1 cup fresh spinach | $0.50

few dashes nutmeg | $1.50 for 1 ounce

directions | Serves 2

1. Heat olive oil in a medium frying pan over medium heat. Add onions and cook for 3-5 minutes, until very fragrant and lightly browned. Remove from pan and set aside.

2. Lay a tortilla on a clean, dry surface and spread with half of the smashed squash. Sprinkle with salt and pepper and top with half of the cheese, half of the spinach, and half of the onions. Top with a dash of nutmeg and a second tortilla. Press gently to adhere. Repeat with the remaining quesadilla ingredients so you have two assembled quesadillas.

3. Heat the remaining olive oil in the pan you used to cook the onions. Cook the quesadillas, one at a time over medium heat, for 2-3 minutes on each side, or until tortillas are brown and crispy and the cheese has melted.

4. Cut into wedges and serve immediately.

PASS ME A QUESADILLA,

WOULD YOU, PUMPKIN?

grilled tofu sandwiches with lemon aioli

I always forget how much I like tofu as a sandwich filling. I think of it for stir-fries and curries but somehow sandwiches fall off my tofu radar. Thank goodness I remembered because this one is a winner.

This meaty grilled tofu preparation is one that even the most finicky carnivore will crave. Vegans can easily sub soy mayonnaise for the regular stuff.

I highly (like, highly) recommend serving these with sweet potato fries.

PREP TIME 0:10 | COOK TIME 0:10

ingredients | Total Cost $7.50

2 tablespoons extra-virgin olive oil plus more for the pan | Pantry

4 tablespoons balsamic vinegar | Pantry

leaves from 1 sprig fresh rosemary, chopped | $1 for a bunch

2 cloves garlic, minced, divided | Pantry

salt and pepper to taste | Pantry

8 ounces firm tofu, sliced into 3 x3-inch squares, about $1/4$ inch thick | $1.50 for 14 ounces

$1/2$ red onion, sliced | 0.50

2 sandwich rolls (I'm fond of Earth Grains Thin Buns) | $3 for 8 rolls

3 tablespoons mayonnaise | Pantry

juice of $1/2$ lemon | $0.50

1 handful fresh baby spinach | $1 for 2 cups

directions | Makes 2 sandwiches

1. Marinade: Combine olive oil, balsamic vinegar, rosemary, one minced clove of garlic, salt, and pepper to taste in a bowl and mix well.

2. Place sliced tofu in a shallow pan or baking dish and cover with marinade. Cover with plastic wrap and refrigerate for fifteen minutes.

3. Once tofu has marinated, heat a grill or grill pan over medium-high heat and brush with olive oil. Grill tofu and onions (at the same time if the grill/pan is big enough) until charred on both sides. Add salt to taste if needed.

4. Toast the sandwich buns if desired.

5. Mix together the remaining garlic clove, mayonnaise, lemon juice, and salt and pepper to taste. Spread on both sides of each bun.

6. To assemble the sandwiches, divide the spinach, tofu, and grilled onions between the buns. Serve warm.

spanakopita burgers

These luscious burgers were born when I woke up one morning craving spanakopita, but alas, had no phyllo. I did, however, have spinach, onion, garlic, and feta. Ground beef, I decided, would accommodate these Greek flavors.

The process was easy (certainly much easier than working with fragile, flaky, and sometimes unbelievably frustrating phyllo dough . . .)—just a matter of mixing the ingredients with my hands and then forming patties to grill. The results? Slightly melted feta oozing out of tender and extremely flavorful burgers (which, thanks to the addition of olive oil turned pleasantly crisp on the outside). Additionally, thanks to all the extra ingredients, these burgers are BIG and quite filling. Chopped chard or kale would make a nice stand-in for the spinach and roasted red peppers or whole cherry tomatoes make a nice addition.

PREP TIME 0:15 | COOK TIME 0:08

ingredients | Total Cost $10.50

1 pound lean ground beef | $3.50

¼ teaspoon salt | Pantry

several good grinds black pepper | Pantry

1 egg, lightly beaten | $1.50 for 12

1 tablespoon extra-virgin olive oil, plus more for brushing the grill or grill pan | Pantry

2-3 cloves garlic, chopped | Pantry

¼ medium onion, finely chopped | $0.50 for a whole onion

1 handful fresh flat-leaf parsley leaves, chopped | $1 for a bunch

1 cup (packed) fresh spinach leaves (kale or chard also work well), chopped | $1 for a bunch

4 ounces feta cheese, crumbled | $3

directions | Serves 4

1. Combine all ingredients in a mixing bowl and use hands to combine well. Form mixture into four patties and transfer to a clean plate.

2. Lightly brush a grill or grill pan with olive oil and heat over medium heat. Cook burgers to desired done-ness (cut one open to check if it's cooked enough for you) and serve immediately.

green apple-goat cheese sandwiches

Luna Park in San Francisco is one of my favorite neighborhood restaurants. Nice enough for a date, casual enough for a regular weeknight dinner, with great cocktails and a fun modern take on classic comfort food. (Oh, and if you follow Luna Park on Twitter, you'll see that they're super generous with discounts and coupons.)

Nearly every time I go, I order the Warm Goat Cheese Fondue with Grilled Bread and Sliced Apples—a little pot of bubbling goat cheese with crisp Granny Smith apples, sliced thinly enough to be delicate and thickly enough to hold all the gooey goat cheese goodness and crusty pieces of ciabatta that have been lightly charred on the grill. So. Freaking. Delicious.

On a recent visit, it occurred to me that these flavors might work nicely together in a sandwich, and, well . . . I was right.

PREP TIME 0:10 | COOK TIME 0:08

ingredients | Total Cost $8

4 slices good sandwich bread (I like sourdough) | $2.50 for a loaf

3 ounces soft, spreadable goat cheese at room temperature | $3.50 for 4 ounces

salt and pepper to taste | Pantry

1 Granny Smith apple, sliced very thin | $0.50

2 tablespoons unsalted butter at room temperature | $1.50 for a stick

directions | Makes 2 sandwiches

1. Spread all four slices of bread with the goat cheese. Place the apple slices on two of the bread slices, top with salt and pepper and cover each with the remaining two slices of goat cheese-spread bread.

2. Spread the outsides of the sandwiches with the butter. Set aside.

3. Heat a frying pan over medium heat. Grill sandwiches for 3-4 minutes on each side, or until the bread is golden-brown and crisp.

4. Serve warm, sliced on the diagonal.

shrimp-vegetable quesadillas

The perfect cure for the common quesadilla, this satisfying dish is filling enough to be dinner in itself, but sometimes I cut it into smaller wedges and serve it as an appetizer. Feel free to switch up the vegetables as the seasons change. It's equally great with asparagus in the summer and roasted butternut squash in the fall.

PREP TIME 0:15 | COOK TIME 0:15

ingredients | Total Cost $13

2 tablespoons extra-virgin olive oil, divided | Pantry

1 white onion, half sliced into thin rounds, half diced | $0.50

1 carrot, sliced on the bias | $0.50

1 red bell pepper, thinly sliced | $1

8 large raw shrimp, deveined, tails removed, and cut into 1-inch pieces | $4

2 large flour tortillas | $3 for twelve

1 cup Monterey jack cheese | $3 for 8 ounces

2 cups baby spinach | $1

salt and pepper to taste | Pantry

directions | Serves 2

1. Heat 1 tablespoon olive oil in a cast-iron or grill pan over medium-high heat. Add sliced onions and allow to brown slightly. Turn onions over and add carrots and bell peppers. Cook for 4-5 minutes or until carrots soften slightly. Add shrimp and cook slightly until just pink and firm. Season well with salt and pepper. Remove from heat and set aside.

2. Heat remaining olive oil in a large frying pan over high heat. While oil heats, assemble quesadillas by laying a tortilla on a clean, flat surface. Sprinkle with half of the cheese, half of the spinach, and half of the vegetable-shrimp mixture. Fold in half. Repeat with remaining tortilla and fillings. Fry the quesadillas one or two at a time, depending on the size of your pan for 2-3 minutes on each side or until golden-brown and crisp.

3. To serve, cut the quesadillas into wedges.

hipster dogs

When I think of hipsters, I think of skinny black jeans, pretentiousness, bad haircuts, and sausages. Yes, sausages. Think about it—sausages are just unclassy enough to seem ironic (hipsters like doing anything ironically), yet overpriced gourmet sausages abound (hipsters also like spending money unnecessarily). Plus any hipster bar worth its salt is within walking distance of a good late-night sausage cart. And not that I'm suggesting anything, but this dish is easy enough that it could probably be thrown together fairly successfully after a night of binge-drinking cheap beer.

PREP TIME 0:05 | COOK TIME 0:07

ingredients | Total Cost $13.50

2 grilling sausages, any kind | $4 for a four-pack

1 teaspoon olive oil | Pantry

2 sprouted-grain hot dog buns | $3 for six

fancy mustard (I like sweet-hot) | $3

¼ cup shredded Muenster, jack or other semi-soft cheese | $3

¼ onion, diced | $0.50

directions | Makes 2 dogs

1. Split the sausages in half lengthwise. Heat the olive oil in a grill pan over high heat. Cook the sausages for 2-3 minutes on each side until plump, with grill-marks on both sides.

2. While the sausages cook, split the buns and toast them in the toaster oven or regular oven (at about 400°F). Once toasted, spread with mustard.

3. Assemble the sausages in the hot dog buns and top with the cheese and onions. Place the assembled dogs under a broiler set to high (this can also be done in a small toaster oven) for 1-2 minutes or until the cheese is melted.

bbq pork burgers

I love grilling, but I get tired of the same old hot dogs and hamburgers over and over again. With this in mind, I set out to create a simple-to-make, yet unique burger. These ultra-easy ones satisfy a craving for pulled pork, but can be made in the same amount of time it takes to assemble a ground beef burger patty.

Note: The burgers can also be rolled into smaller balls and baked as individual meatballs.

PREP TIME 0:10 | COOK TIME 0:15

ingredients | Total Cost $11

1 pound ground pork | $3.50

2 cloves garlic, minced | Pantry

3 scallions, chopped | $1 for a bunch

4 tablespoons prepared sauce, plus more for serving | $4 for an 18-ounce bottle

$\frac{1}{2}$ cup breadcrumbs | $2.50 for 12 ounces

vegetable or canola oil for grill/grill pan | Pantry

directions | Makes 4 burgers

1. Combine pork, garlic, scallions, BBQ sauce, and bread crumbs in a mixing bowl. Use hands to combine well, then form into four patties.

2. Lightly oil a grill or grill pan over medium-high heat. Cook burgers to desired doneness, brushing with extra BBQ sauce once or twice during cooking.

3. Serve on buns, over mixed greens or plain.

chicken mango flautas with lime crema

My friend, Brett and I regularly meet at Chilango, a Mexican restaurant in San Francisco's Mission District, both because of its delicious food and of its being equidistant to our respective apartments. One night, we caught up over a carafe of sweet sangria and a platter of the most amazing crispy duck flautas, drizzled with Mexican crema and topped with a pile of fresh green cabbage.

I wanted to recreate it, but duck can be a little pricey, so I substituted pan-cooked chicken thighs (the opposite of pricey). I made them my own by adding a bit with fresh mango and jalapeño. Serve these with a bowl of fresh guacamole.

PREP TIME 0:30 | COOK TIME 0:10

ingredients | Total Cost $7

vegetable oil for frying | Pantry

¹/₂ pound boneless, skinless chicken thighs | $3

1 mango, peeled, pitted, and finely chopped | $1.50

1 jalapeño, (seeds intact—take 'em out if you don't like spicy), finely chopped | $0.25

salt to taste | Pantry

8 (6-inch) corn tortillas | $1 for 12

3 tablespoons sour cream | $1 for 4 ounces

juice of ¹/₂ lime | $0.25

¹/₄ green cabbage, cored and thinly sliced | $0.50

directions | Makes 8 flautas

1. Heat 2 teaspoons vegetable oil in a large frying pan over high heat. Cook chicken thighs for 4-5 minutes on each side, or until cooked through. Remove from heat and cool for five minutes. Use a fork and knife to shred the chicken thighs into bite-size pieces. Combine in a bowl with the mango, jalapeno, and a pinch of salt.

2. Heat about ¹/₂-inch vegetable oil in the frying pan over high heat (no need to rinse it first).

3. While oil heats, microwave the tortillas for 20-30 seconds to make them very pliable. Once tortillas are cool enough to handle, fill each one with 2-3 tablespoon of the chicken-mango mixture.

4. Carefully lace rolled flautas into the oil, seam-side down, working in batches. Cook for 1-2 minutes on each side, or until golden-brown and crispy. Drain on paper towels.

5. Whisk the lime juice into the sour cream. Set aside.

6. To serve the flautas, place them on a plate or plates. Drizzle the sour cream mixture over the top. Heap a small pile of cabbage atop.

easy molasses pulled pork sandwiches

I love pulled pork, but have been hesitant to make it at home because every recipe I've found calls for 5-7 hours of slow braising in the oven. I don't know about you, but I haven't had 5-7 hours to spare since, like, 1997.

But I got to thinking, and it occurred to me that I could probably apply the same quick stovetop braising technique I used with Pan-Braised Chipotle Short Ribs to pork shoulder to make it tender enough to shred. It worked like a charm in this perky-sweet sauce.

I whipped up some quick and light coleslaw by tossing thinly sliced green cabbage with some Creamy Yogurt-Herb Dressing and served the pulled pork piled with slaw on soft wholegrain buns.

PREP TIME 0:20 | COOK TIME 1:30

ingredients | Total Cost $16.25

2 tablespoons vegetable or olive oil | Pantry

1 red onion, sliced | $0.50

4 cloves garlic, minced | Pantry

2 pounds pork stew meat (cubed pork shoulder) | $9

3 large tomatoes, diced | $1.50

1 green jalapeño, finely diced | $0.25

1 quart chicken, beef, or vegetable stock | $2

3 tablespoons molasses | $3 for 10 ounces

¼ cup brown sugar | Pantry

freshly cracked pepper | Pantry

directions | Serves 4

1. Heat the oil over medium heat in a large soup pot (make sure it has a fitted lid) or Dutch oven. Add onion and garlic and cook until fragrant, about 2 minutes.

2. Add pork pieces to the pan and brown, about 1 minute on each side.

3. Add diced tomatoes, jalapeño, and stock. Stir well to combine.

4. Gently stir in molasses, brown sugar, and a few grinds of black pepper.

5. Cover pot with lid and cook for and hour (up to an hour-and-a-half), until liquid has been reduced to a thick sauce and meat is very tender.

6. Use two forks to pull pork into shreds.

7. Serve pulled pork on sandwich buns with coleslaw, or on its own.

pupusas with cheese

I have loved Salvadoran pupusas (stuffed corn tortillas) for a long time, and yet had yet to make them until recently. Upon tasting my first batch (and, um, there have been three since yesterday afternoon . . .) I couldn't get over how scrumptious they were, especially considering how easy they were to make. The tortilla-forming takes a bit of practice, but have faith—you'll get it quickly.

The first time I made them, I stuck with simple, classic cheese filling as shown here. The second and third times, however, I got more creative, filling them once with black beans and cheese and again with roasted vegetables. Feel free to experiment.

Note: To make the classic cabbage slaw shown here that pupusas are often served with, simply toss together ½ cabbage, thinly sliced, juice of 1 lime, 1 tablespoon extra virgin olive oil, 1 handful fresh cilantro, chopped, salt, and pepper to taste.

PREP TIME 0:20 | COOK TIME 0:15

ingredients | Total cost $5.50

4 cups masa harina | $2 for 1 pound

pinch of salt | Pantry

2 cups water

2 cups shredded Monterey jack or queso blanco | $3.50 for 8 ounces

directions | Makes 4 pupusas

1. Mix masa harina, salt, and water together in a bowl to make a sticky dough (add a touch more water if it's too crumbly after stirring well). Divide the dough into eight balls.

2. Place a ball between two pieces of wax paper and roll out, using hands or a rolling pin, into a 6-inch circle. Set on a plate coated lightly with masa harina. Repeat with remaining balls of dough.

3. To assemble a pupusa, place ¼ cup shredded cheese on top of one dough round. Spread out evenly. Top with a second dough round and pinch edges gently to seal. Repeat with remaining dough and cheese.

4. To cook, heat an ungreased griddle or pan (preferably cast-iron) over high heat. Cook the pupusas for 2-3 minutes on each side, or until lightly charred in places.

5. Serve hot, with cabbage slaw and salsa if desired.

classy cheesesteaks

Upon perusing a Google search of "Philly cheesesteak," I was horrified to learn that a secret ingredient in many traditional Philly cheesesteak recipes is Cheez Whiz. Well, if you're looking for that sort of thing, I guess you can feel free to add it to this recipe, but you won't find me sinking my teeth into a hearty, fake cheese-laden cheesesteak. I'm an open-minded girl, but there are few things I hate more than Cheez Whiz (or any aerosol cheese for that matter—come on! Cheese in a can?). Call me a snob, I don't care. Just keep it away from me.

These cheesesteaks keep it classy with provolone. Jack or fontina would be good, too.

PREP TIME 0:15 | COOK TIME 0:05

ingredients | Total Cost $9.50

2 teaspoons olive oil | Pantry

1 small white onion, thinly sliced | $0.50

1 red bell pepper, thinly sliced | $1

2 cloves garlic, minced | Pantry

¹/₂ pound thinly sliced sirloin, preferably grass-fed | $4

salt and pepper to taste | Pantry

4 slices provolone | $2

2 sourdough or Italian sandwich rolls, split lengthwise | $2

directions | Makes 2 large sandwiches

1. Heat olive oil in a large frying pan, preferably cast-iron over high heat. Add onion, bell pepper, and garlic and cook for 1-2 minutes or until onions soften and become fragrant. Add sirloin and cook for another 1-2 minutes, stirring frequently, until beef is no longer pink. Season mixture with salt and pepper to taste.

2. Top entire mixture with cheese slices and allow to melt, stirring slightly to coax melting. Spoon cheesy mixture into split rolls and serve immediately.

bulgur-cashew veggie burgers

I love, love, love nutty, high-fiber bulgur. Such a great alternative to brown rice or couscous, and so versatile! Here, I use it as a base for these healthy veggie burgers. Tuck them into pita pockets, serve them on whole wheat buns or do like I do and eat them on their own, topped with spicy aioli and a few slices of fresh tomato.

PREP TIME 0:45 | COOK TIME 0:15

ingredients | Total Cost $12.75

1 tablespoon extra virgin olive oil, plus more for grill | Pantry

1 onion, finely chopped, divided | $0.50

¹/₂ cup uncooked bulgur | $3 for 14 ounces

1 tablespoon soy sauce | Pantry

¹/₂ cup raw cashews | $2.50 for 8 ounces

4 cloves garlic, minced, divided | Pantry

1 handful fresh cilantro leaves, chopped | $1 for a bunch

1 teaspoon ground cumin | $1.50 for 1 ounce

1 cup canned pinto beans, rinsed and drained | $1 for a 14-ounce can

¹/₃ cup frozen green peas | $1.50 for a 10-ounce bag

¹/₄ cup bread crumbs | $1.50 for 14 ounces

salt and pepper to taste | Pantry

¹/₄ cup mayonnaise (light is fine) | Pantry

1 jalapeño, seeded, minced | $0.25

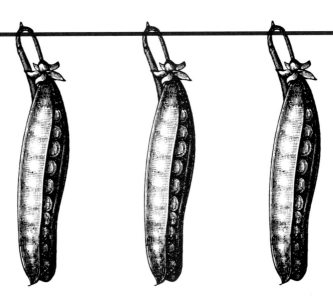

directions | Serves 4

1. Heat olive oil in a medium pot over medium heat. Add onion and cook for 1-2 minutes, just until translucent and fragrant. Add bulgur and 1 cup of water and cook, covered, over low heat until water is absorbed, 10-12 minutes. Stir in soy sauce.

2. Place bulgur mixture, cashews, 2 cloves of the garlic, cilantro, and cumin in a food processor and pulse, just until blended. Transfer to a mixing bowl.

3. Mash beans with the back of a fork so they are soft but slightly chunky and stir into bulgur mixture. Add the remaining onion, the peas, the bread crumbs and salt and pepper to taste. Mix well.

4. Form rounded $^1/_2$ cups of mixture into four patties. Chill for at least 20 minutes, or as long as overnight (this is the key—if you skip this step the burgers will crumble).

5. While the burgers chill, whisk together the remaining garlic, mayonnaise, and jalapeño. Season with salt and pepper to taste and set aside.

6. Brush a grill or grill pan with olive oil and heat over medium heat. Grill the burgers for 4-5 minutes on each side, or until charred and lightly crisp on the outside.

7. Serve on buns if desired (I like them on their own, with greens), topped with the aioli and tomato slices. Serve immediately.

spicy fried-chicken sando

So, I had set out to recreate the fried chicken sandwich from Bakesale Betty in the Temescal neighborhood of Oakland, CA. Known far and wide as the best fried chicken sandwich in the Bay Area, the sandwich has many fans, including yours truly, but schlepping from San Francisco to Oakland for a sandwich is hard for me to justify . . . so I decided to figure out how to make it at home. I found the exact recipe for Betty's sandwich online, and then set about tinkering. I followed the recipe I found loosely and added my own personal (read: spicy) touches. Rather than fully deep-frying my chicken, I did a nice shallow fry (still not good for you, but better). Instead of the traditional red wine vinaigrette, I made a spicy, creamy dressing for my slaw and topped it all with some spicy, crunchy jalapeño rings. Y-U-M.

PREP TIME 1:00 (including soaking) | COOK TIME 0:08

ingredients | Total Cost $16

2 boneless, skinless chicken breasts | $5

2 cups buttermilk (regular or low-fat) | $1.50 for a quart

1 cup flour | Pantry

1 teaspoon cayenne pepper | $1.50 for 1 ounce

salt and pepper | Pantry

2 tablespoons rice vinegar | $2 for 10 ounces

1/4 cup mayonnaise | Pantry

2 teaspoons sugar or honey | Pantry

2 teaspoons Sriracha or other Asian chili sauce (more/less to taste) | $2.50 for 17 ounces

1/2 head green cabbage, cored and thinly sliced | $1

1/2 red onion, finely chopped | $0.50

1 carrot, shredded | $0.25

1 handful fresh cilantro leaves, chopped | $1

vegetable or canola oil | Pantry

2 very fresh French or other sandwich rolls | $1

1 green jalapeño, sliced into rings | $0.25

directions | Makes 2 large sandwiches or 4 small sandwiches

1. Slice the chicken breasts into "tenders"—strips that are 4-5 inches long and about 2 inches wide. Place in a shallow bowl or baking dish and cover with the buttermilk. Cover tightly with plastic wrap and refrigerate for an hour or up to overnight (I tried both and the overnight soaking yielded knee-bucklingly tender chicken).

2. While the chicken soaks, get everything ready: combine the flour, cayenne, and 1 teaspoon each of salt and pepper in a wide, shallow dish. Mix well and set aside.

3. Whisk together the rice vinegar, mayonnaise, sugar or honey, Sriracha, and salt and pepper to taste. Set aside.

4. In a mixing bowl, toss together the cabbage, onion, carrot, and cilantro. Pour the dressing over the mixture and toss well. Refrigerate until ready to use.

5. Once the chicken has finished soaking, remove it from the buttermilk and place it on a clean plate. Sprinkle generously with salt and pepper.

6. Place the soaked chicken and the prepared flour mixture next to the stove.

7. Prepare the oil by pouring about 1 inch of oil into a large frying pan. Heat over medium-high heat until oil becomes very viscous and begins to bubble.

8. To make the chicken, dredge a piece of the chicken in the flour mixture, shake off the excess and carefully drop the chicken into the hot oil. Fry the chicken in small batches for 2-3 minutes on each side, or until golden-brown and crispy, using tongs to flip. Drain on paper towels and sprinkle just-fried chicken lightly with salt.

9. To assemble the sandwiches, split the rolls and top the bottom halves with a few pieces of chicken. Top with a heaping pile of slaw and a few slices of jalapeño. Serve immediately.

lamb-feta burgers with lemon-dill yogurt sauce

This meal was inspired by a lamb burger I had at one of my all-time favorite restaurants in San Francisco, The Monk's Kettle. These burgers are so good I doubt you'll be able to eat just one, which is lucky because they're little. They're also delicious minus the pita and sauce, over a bed of spinach dressed with olive oil and lemon juice.

PREP TIME 0:25 | COOK TIME 0:10

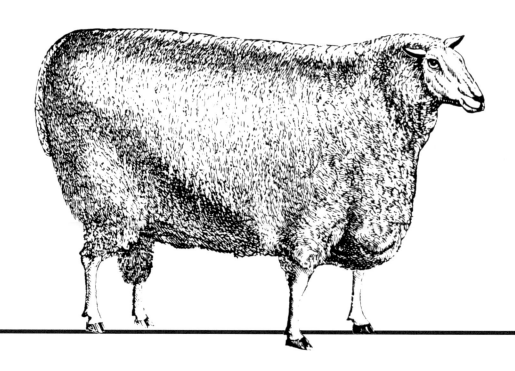

ingredients | Total Cost $17.50

¹/₂ pound lean ground lamb | $5

¹/₂ red onion, finely diced | $0.50

1 small bunch flat-leaf parsley, chopped | $1

2 ounces crumbled feta cheese | $4 for 6 ounces

3 teaspoons extra-virgin olive oil, divided, plus more for pan | Pantry

3 cloves garlic, finely chopped, divided | Pantry

¹/₄ cup Greek yogurt (any percent fat) | $2 for 6 ounces

juice and zest of ¹/₂ lemon | $0.50

¹/₄ teaspoon dried dill | $1.50 for 1 ounce

salt and pepper to taste | Pantry

4 small pita rounds, halved | $2 for ten

1 cup fresh spinach leaves | $1

directions | Makes 8 mini-burgers

1. Combine lamb, onion, parsley, feta, 2 teaspoons olive oil, 2 cloves garlic and ¹/₂ teaspoon each of salt and pepper in a mixing bowl. Very gently use clean hands to combine all ingredients, being careful not to break the feta down. Form into eight patties, about $2\frac{1}{2}$ inches wide. Set patties on a clean plate.

2. Lightly brush a grill pan, regular pan or grill with enough olive oil to lightly grease it. Cook burgers to desired done-ness (I like medium rare: 2-3 minutes on each side). Remove from heat.

3. Whisk together the yogurt with remaining minced clove of garlic, 1 teaspoon olive oil, lemon juice, dill, and salt and pepper to taste.

4. To serve the burgers, place a small handful of spinach into each pita pocket. Place a burger in with the spinach and drizzle with the yogurt sauce. Serve immediately.

TURKEY BURGERS: LEAN,

MEAN AND LOVELY.

basil-feta turkeyburgers

My brother Jeremy and his girlfriend, Holly, declared this my best recipe ever. As such, they cook these burgers together at least once a week, and for good reason: these easy burgers taste much fancier than they actually are. The key is to use fresh basil though— not dried, as it imparts a bright, sunny flavor. Also make sure to use ripe, flavorful tomatoes. When tomatoes aren't in season, try these with $1/2$ cup chopped sundried tomatoes instead.

Another great benefit of these is that, by mixing in additional ingredients, you are able to stretch a mere $1/2$ pound of ground meat into four burgers.

PREP TIME 0:25 | COOK TIME 0:12

ingredients | Total Cost $13.50

$1/2$ **pound lean ground turkey** | $3

1 Roma tomato, chopped | $0.50

1 small bunch basil, chopped | $1

3 ounces crumbled feta cheese | $4 for 8 ounces

2 cloves garlic, minced | Pantry

$1/2$ **red onion, chopped** | $0.50

generous pinch each of salt and pepper | Pantry

olive oil (for brushing grill or grill pan) | Pantry

4 hamburger buns | $3 for six

1 avocado, sliced | $1.50

directions | Makes 4 burgers

1. Combine turkey, tomato, basil, feta, garlic, onion, salt, and pepper in a mixing bowl. Use hands to mix and form into four patties. Transfer to a clean plate. Wash hands thoroughly.

2. Heat a grill or grill pan over high heat. Brush lightly with oil.

3. Grill burgers for 4-6 minutes on each side or until lightly charred and fully cooked.

4. Serve on burgers with avocado.

chipotle cheddar burgers with cilantro aioli

These are, in my opinion, the ultimate summer burger, though I cook them year round on my little cast-iron grill pan. I like them bun-less, topped with fresh avocado and a big, ripe slice of tomato.

PREP TIME 0:15 | COOK TIME 0:10

ingredients | Total Cost $11.50

1 pound lean ground beef | $4.50

¹/₂ white onion, finely chopped | $0.50

4 cloves garlic, finely minced, divided | Pantry

1 chipotle pepper (canned in adobo), finely chopped, plus 1-2 spoonfuls of the sauce it comes packed in | $2 for a 6-ounce can

6 ounces medium or sharp cheddar, cut into ¹/₂-inch cubes | $3.50 for 8 ounces

salt and ground pepper | Pantry

¹/₄ cup mayonnaise | Pantry

1 handful fresh cilantro leaves, very finely chopped | $1 for a bunch

directions | Serves 4

1. Preheat grill to medium-high. Oil or spray lightly to avoid sticking.

2. In a mixing bowl, combine beef, onion, 2 cloves garlic, the chipotle pepper and sauce, the chopped cheddar and ¹/₂ teaspoon each of salt and pepper. Mix well using your hands.

3. Shape the mixture into four patties and grill for 3-4 minutes on each side (at least long enough to melt the cheese).

4. While the burgers cook, whisk together the remaining garlic, mayonnaise, cilantro, and salt and pepper to taste. Set aside.

5. Serve the burgers on buns if desired, or on their own, topped with a dollop of the aioli.

chapter

6

strands, elbows, and angel hair

Ahh, pasta. The ultimate starving student food. It needs little more than a slick of extra virgin olive oil, some chopped garlic and a sprinkle of salt and pepper to be palatable, but the possibilities for pasta are endless. Trader Joes often carries good imported Italian pasta for a mere $0.99 per bag, but even if you don't have access to a Trader Joes, your local grocery store will likely sell pasta for not much more. Buy it on sale and keep it in your pantry so you're always ready when hunger strikes.

Another good pasta sub, as you'll see in some of these recipes, is to use Chinese wonton wrappers (usually sold refrigerated near the tofu, or frozen) or fresh Chinese wheat noodles. They're essentially identical to fresh pasta (but much, much cheaper).

best mac and cheese with parmesan crust

This is my absolute best macaroni and cheese recipe. At least according to my palate, the seasonings are just right and the consistency is creamy enough to accomplish the comforting that macaroni and cheese is supposed to—without making my dinner guests pass out in a cheesy-carb coma. Mac and cheese makes a tasty meal on its own, but I like to serve it alongside grilled sausages and a green salad.

PREP TIME 0:25 | COOK TIME 0:25

ingredients | Total Cost $15

2 tablespoons unsalted butter, plus more for the pan | $1.50 for a stick

8 ounces macaroni elbows (or regular macaroni elbows) | $1 for 16 ounces

2 tablespoons flour | Pantry

1 cup milk (low-fat or whole) | $1.50 for a pint

1/4 teaspoon nutmeg | $1.50 for 1 ounce

1 1/2 cups shredded sharp cheddar cheese | $3.50 for 10 ounces

salt and pepper to taste | Pantry

1/2 cup shredded Parmesan cheese | $4 for 10 ounces

directions | Serves 4–6

1. Preheat oven to 375°F. Lightly butter a large rectangular casserole pan or 4-6 individual ovenproof dishes (such as small soufflé dishes).

2. Cook pasta in salted boiling water according to directions. Drain, return to pot, and set aside.

3. In a medium pot, melt butter over medium-high heat. Sprinkle in flour until a sticky dough forms. Cook dough, whisking constantly, for 1-2 minutes.

4. Slowly pour in milk until a thick white sauce forms, continuing to whisk. Whisk in nutmeg. Gradually add cheese, and whisk until smooth. Add salt and pepper to taste and cook for an additional 1-2 minutes, continuing to whisk.

5. Use a spatula to scrape all of the sauce into the cooked pasta and stir gently until all pasta is coated. Transfer pasta-cheese mixture into the prepared pan(s) and top with shredded Parmesan.

6. Bake for 25-30 minutes or until cheese on top bubbles. Serve hot.

truffled mac and cheese

Truffles, usually considered off-limits in my BrokeAss kitchen, make this simple macaroni and cheese recipe decadent and unique, thanks to Trader Joes' very reasonably priced Italian Truffle Cheese. I skip a bread-crumb topping so as not to overpower the truffles' subtlety, and serve it with just a whisper of freshly ground black pepper.

PREP TIME 0:20 | COOK TIME 0:15

ingredients | Total Cost $9.50

8 ounces elbow macaroni | $1 for 16 ounces

2 tablespoons unsalted butter, plus more for pan/ramekins | $1 for a stick

2 tablespoons all-purpose flour | Pantry

1 cup whole milk | $1.50 for a pint

5 ounces Italian truffle cheese, shredded | $6 for 8 ounces

salt to taste | Pantry

directions | Serves 4

1. Preheat broiler on high. Lightly butter four oven-proof bowls/large ramekins or one 8-inch baking pan.

2. Cook macaroni according to package directions. Drain and return to pot.

3. While macaroni cooks, melt butter in a medium pot over medium heat. Whisk in flour until a sticky dough forms. Very slowly add milk, whisking constantly, until a creamy white sauce forms. Add shredded truffle cheese, whisking to encourage melting. Once all cheese has melted, remove from heat and season with salt to taste.

4. Pour cheese sauce over cooked pasta and use a rubber scraper to combine well.

5. Scrape macaroni and cheese sauce into prepared bowls/ramekins/pan. Place under broiler, just until a very light golden-brown crust forms on top.

6. Serve hot.

brown butter pumpkin mac and cheese

Pumpkin adds an earthy richness to dishes, plus lots of fiber, few calories and zero fat. Since I'm constantly reinventing mac and cheese, I figured I might as well try it with pumpkin.

The result was a creamy, satisfying mac with a rich sauce that will make you want to lick your plate. Brown butter, aged white cheddar, and nutmeg perfectly complement autumnal pumpkin and taste so rich, you will forget that this dish has less than half of the fat and calories of regular mac and cheese.

PREP TIME 0:15 | COOK TIME 0:22

ingredients | Total Cost $9.50

8 ounces elbow macaroni, penne, shells, or other small pasta shape | $1 for 16 ounces

2 tablespoons unsalted butter plus more for the pan | $1 for a stick

2 tablespoons all-purpose flour | Pantry

³/₄ cup milk (any kind) | $1 for a pint

³/₄ cup unsweetened canned pumpkin | $1.50 for a 15-ounce can

¹/₂ cup plus 2 tablespoons shredded aged white cheddar cheese | $3.50 for 8 ounces

dash nutmeg | $1.50 for 1 ounce

salt and pepper to taste | Pantry

directions | Serves 4

1. Preheat oven to 375°F.

2. Lightly butter an 11 x 13-inch baking pan or four ramekins/oven-proof bowls.

3. Cook macaroni in salted boiling water according to package directions.

4. While macaroni cooks, melt the butter in a medium pot over medium heat. As soon as it begins to brown, add the flour and whisk until you have a very sticky dough.

5. Slowly whisk in the milk to form a creamy white sauce.

6. Continue whisking as you add the pumpkin and ¹/₂ cup of the white cheddar. You should have a very creamy orange sauce. Season with nutmeg, salt, and pepper.

7. Drain the pasta and return it to its pot. Use a rubber spatula to scrape all of the sauce over the pasta and stir to coat the pasta evenly.

8. Scrape the sauced pasta into the prepared pan(s) and top with the reserved cheddar plus more salt and pepper.

9. Bake for 18-22 minutes or until the cheese is very bubbly and lightly browned on top. Serve hot.

summer capellini with red pepper sauce

Some people like to put fake sugar, butter substitutes, and other weird stuff in their food to keep it light. I prefer to simply use a little creativity.

Red bell peppers become incredibly creamy and decadent after being roasted and pureed with garlic, onions, and just a smidgen of half-and-half. I added shredded carrots, fresh corn, and tomatoes because that's what I had in my vegetable bin, but feel free to use spinach, broccoli, mushrooms, eggplant—whatever you have on hand. I like to leave the veggies raw, letting the heat of the pasta and sauce gently "cook" them. If you prefer softer veggies, feel free to blanch them before adding them to the pasta.

PREP TIME 0:25 | COOK TIME 0:20

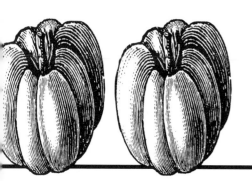

ingredients | Total Cost $7

¹/₂ pound capellini (angel hair) pasta, preferably whole wheat or Dreamfields | $2.50 for 1 pound

1 red bell pepper | $1

1 tablespoon extra-virgin olive oil | Pantry

¹/₂ onion, diced | $0.50

2 cloves garlic, minced | Pantry

¹/₈ cup half-and-half | $1.50 for 1 ounce

2 carrots, shredded | $0.50

1 ripe tomato, diced | $0.50

1 large handful fresh basil leaves, chopped | $1 for a bunch

salt and pepper to taste | Pantry

directions | Serves 4

1. Cook capellini in boiling water according to directions. Drain and set aside.

2. While capellini cooks, roast the red pepper, either over a flame on a gas burner or under a broiler in the oven. Hold pepper (using tongs, or a baking pan if using a broiler), directly over (or under) the flame, rotating periodically, until its skin is completely blackened. Rinse pepper under cool water and peel away the blackened skin, revealing a very soft, silky pepper. Remove stem and seeds. Chop pepper into small pieces.

3. Heat olive oil in a small pot over medium heat. Add onion and garlic and cook just until fragrant, 1-2 minutes. Add red pepper, half-and-half, and 3 tablespoon water. Cook until liquid begins to bubble, 2-3 minutes. Remove from heat.

4. Puree pepper mixture, using a blender, food processor or immersion blender until smooth.

5. Toss pasta with red pepper sauce, vegetables, and basil. Season with salt and pepper.

6. Serve hot.

spaghetti carbonara

Admittedly, this is not a healthy dish, but once in a while, especially if you are seriously lacking time and cash, it can be a glorious treat.

It's decadent on its own, but nice add-ins include red pepper flakes, chopped fresh flat-leaf parsley, frozen green peas (they'll defrost once they come into contact with the fresh pasta), broccoli florets, sautéed mushrooms, spinach or chard.

Also, don't worry about bacteria from the raw egg—the heat of the pasta will take care of it.

PREP TIME 0:10 | COOK TIME 0:10

ingredients | Total Cost $7

8 ounces dried spaghetti | $1 for 16 ounces

2 strips raw, uncured bacon | $1

3 cloves garlic, chopped | Pantry

salt and pepper | Pantry

1 egg, lightly beaten | $1.50 for six

½ cup grated Parmesan | $3.50 for 8 ounces

directions | Serves 2

1. Cook spaghetti according to package directions in salted boiling water. Drain, reserving ¼ cup cooking water.

2. Heat a large dry frying pan over medium-high heat. Cook bacon strips for 2-3 minutes on each side, or until brown and crisp. Discard all but 1 tablespoon bacon fat. Drain bacon on paper towels. Chop or crumble bacon.

3. Cook the chopped garlic in the reserved bacon fat over medium heat for 30 seconds, or just until fragrant and season with pepper. Add cooked, drained pasta and reserved cooking liquid and toss together using tongs. Cook for 1 minute or until cooking liquid begins to absorb.

4. Remove from heat and toss thoroughly with egg. Continue tossing pasta with one hand, to avoid scrambling the eggs, and add the Parmesan. Toss well. Add the crumbled bacon, season with salt and pepper to taste (careful with the salt—the bacon is already salty), and serve hot.

BECAUSE BACON REALLY DOES

MAKE EVERYTHING BETTER.

spaghetti with green olive pesto

This is one of those great dishes for people who don't think they can cook, mostly because there is so little actual cooking involved in making it. Can you boil pasta? Can you put some stuff into a food processor and press the "on" button? Yep, thought so.

Check you out—you just made dinner.

PREP TIME 0:20 | COOK TIME 0:08

ingredients | Total Cost $8.50

8 ounces dried spaghetti | $1 for 16 ounces

$1/2$ cup pimento-stuffed green olives | $2.50 for a 10-ounce jar

$1/8$ cup shredded Parmesan cheese | $3.50 for 10 ounces

1 large handful fresh basil leaves, torn into pieces | $1 for a bunch

3 tablespoons extra-virgin olive oil | Pantry

juice and zest of 1 lemon | $0.50

salt and pepper to taste | Pantry

directions | Serves 2–3

1. Cook spaghetti in salted boiling water according to directions. Drain and return to pot.

2. Combine olives, Parmesan, basil, olive oil, lemon, salt, and pepper in a food processor or blender until smooth.

3. Toss cooked spaghetti with the pesto. Garnish with more Parmesan, basil, and olives if desired.

sundried tomato ricotta gnocchi

One time, in college, I made fresh gnocchi for an Italian-American guy I was dating. He stood over me in the kitchen, wrinkling his nose and furrowing his brows at my every move.

"That's not how my mom does it," he'd say. "She doesn't use a food processor. She does it all by hand. And her gnocchi are amazing."

I ignored him and concentrated on the burdensome task at hand of peeling, boiling, and mashing potatoes and mixing them with just enough flour so the dough could be handled— but not so much that it became dense. When the gnocchi were finally complete and we sat down at my lovingly set kitchen table to eat, he took a bite, paused for a long time, and said, "these taste . . . different from my mom's."

Needless to say, it was our last date.

These days, I am wiser in many ways. I no longer date men who compare me to their mothers (to my face, anyway), and I make this quick, easy gnocchi with ricotta instead of laborious potatoes. I've paired these delicious tomato-ricotta dumplings with a simple parsley-garlic sauce, but they'd be great with pesto or marinara too.

PREP TIME 0:25 | COOK TIME 0:05

ingredients | Total Cost $11.50

²/₃ cup ricotta | $4 for 15 ounces

8 sun-dried tomatoes, plus more for garnish | $1

¹/₈ cup grated Parmesan cheese, plus more for garnish | $3 for 4 ounces

1¹/₄ cups flour, plus more as needed | Pantry

1 egg yolk | $1.50 for six eggs

salt and pepper | Pantry

¹/₈ cup olive oil | Pantry

1 small bunch parsley, finely chopped | $1

2 cloves garlic, minced | Pantry

directions | Serves 3–4

1. In a food processor, combine ricotta, sun-dried tomatoes, Parmesan, flour, egg yolk, and a pinch of salt. Pulse to form a sticky dough, adding a bit more flour if necessary. Turn out onto a lightly floured surface. Form dough into several long snakes, about ³/₄ thick. Using a very sharp knife, cut into 1-inch "pillows." Set aside on a clean plate.

2. Bring a large pot of salted water to a light boil over high heat. Add gnocchi, working in batches if necessary, and cook for 4-5 minutes, or until gnocchi float to the surface of the pot. Drain and return to pot.

3. While gnocchi cook, heat olive oil in a small frying pan over medium heat. Add garlic, parsley, salt, and pepper and cook just until garlic is very fragrant, 3-4 minutes. Remove from heat.

4. Toss gnocchi with olive oil mixture and a small handful of Parmesan. Serve garnished with a few sun-dried tomatoes, sliced if necessary.

angel hair with wasabi, peas, and mint

This unique pasta dish is a refreshing, satisfying, and downright sophisticated vegetarian supper.

Hint: Try batting your eyelashes and asking your local sushi joint for extra wasabi the next time you order takeout. They'll likely give it to you for free. Otherwise, look for it near the soy sauce.

PREP TIME 0:25 | COOK TIME 0:05

ingredients | Total Cost $12

8 ounces dried angel hair (capellini) pasta | $1 for 16 ounces

1 cup frozen peas, defrosted and divided | $1.50 for 12 ounces

2 cloves garlic | Pantry

2 handfuls of fresh mint leaves | $1

⅓ cup extra-virgin olive oil | Pantry

2 teaspoons prepared wasabi | $3 for 4 ounces

4 ounces crumbled feta | $4 for 8 ounces

1 teaspoon red pepper flakes | $1.50 for 1 ounce

salt and pepper to taste | Pantry

directions | Serves 4

1. Cook pasta according to package directions in salted boiling water. Drain and return to pot.

2. In a food processor, combine half of the peas, mint, garlic, olive oil, and wasabi. Puree until a chunky pesto forms. Season with salt and pepper to taste and toss with hot pasta. Add remaining peas, feta, red pepper flakes, and more salt and pepper if desired.

3. Serve hot, at room temperature, or chilled.

pantry spaghetti

This tasty pasta was invented one weekend after my friend Danny visited from Boston. We spent the weekend traipsing around San Francisco, getting into all kinds of trouble. After he left, I meant to go grocery shopping—I really did . . . but after he left I was just so exhausted from all the fun we had and I just couldn't bring myself to get to the store.

Well sometimes a lack of options forces us to be creative (and thankful for a well-stocked pantry) and the stars align and the resulting dish is truly fantastic, as this one was. Serve it on its own or accompanied by a green salad.

PREP TIME 0:05 | COOK TIME 0:15

ingredients | Total Cost $8.50

8 ounces spaghetti | $1 for 16 ounces

3 tablespoons olive oil | Pantry

3 cloves garlic, chopped | Pantry

1/2 cup bread crumbs | $2

2 teaspoons red pepper flakes | $1.50 for 1 ounce

1/8 cup grated Parmesan | $3

salt and pepper to taste | Pantry

1 small bunch fresh flat leaf parsley, chopped | $1

directions | Serves 2

1. Cook the pasta according to directions in salted water. While the pasta cooks, heat the oil over medium-high heat. Add garlic and cook for about 1 minute, stirring frequently to avoid burning. Add the bread crumbs and stir to combine well with garlic and oil. Allow the crumbs to toast for a few minutes, stirring occasionally.

2. When the pasta has finished cooking, drain it and return it to its pot. Toss with the garlic-breadcrumb mixture, the red pepper flakes, Parmesan, parsley, and salt and pepper.

SHE SELLS SEA SHELLS BY THE
SEA SHORE . . . AND WHEN THAT
GETS OLD, SHE MAKES THESE.

stuffed shells with fresh marinara sauce

This dish is so delicious and perfect in its simplicity. All you need is fresh ricotta and Parmesan, quality pasta, some ripe, flavorful Roma tomatoes, garlic, and basil. If the ingredients are great, you'll find that it's nearly impossible to screw this one up.

PREP TIME 0:25 | COOK TIME 0:30

ingredients | Total Cost $13

8 large pasta shells | $2

6 Roma tomatoes, finely chopped | $3

1 small bunch basil, chopped | $1

4 cloves garlic, minced | Pantry

salt and pepper to taste | Pantry

1 cup ricotta | $4

1/8 cup shredded Parmesan | $3

directions | Serves 2–3

1. Preheat oven to 400°F.

2. Cook shells in salted water according to package directions. Drain and set aside.

3. Combine tomatoes, basil, garlic, salt, and pepper in a bowl. Pour half of the tomato mixture onto the bottom of an 8-inch square pan or pie dish. Reserve the remaining half.

4. Combine ricotta and Parmesan in a small bowl. Season with salt and pepper. Carefully stuff 3-4 tablespoons of the cheese mixture into each shell. Set the shells, open end up, in the tomato mixture in the pan. Cover with the remaining tomato mixture and more basil if desired.

5. Cover the pan tightly with foil and bake for 25-30 minutes. Serve hot.

pumpkin gnocchi with onions and sage

This quintessentially autumnal dish is much easier to make than it looks. Serve as a side dish alongside roast chicken or just on its own.

If you were so inclined, a bit of lightly pan-fried pancetta would be a good addition, but it doesn't need it.

PREP TIME 0:15 | COOK TIME 0:15

ingredients | Total Cost $9.50

½ cup canned pumpkin | $1.50 for a 15 ounce can

½ cup ricotta cheese (I prefer the whole milk kind) | $4 for 14 ounces

1 cup flour, plus more for rolling | Pantry

1 egg | $1.50 for 12

dash of nutmeg (optional)

½ teaspoon salt | Pantry

freshly ground black pepper | Pantry

6 tablespoon butter | $1 for a stick

1 medium onion, sliced | $0.50 for a whole onion

6-7 fresh sage leaves | $1 for a bunch

directions | Serves 2–4

1. Set a large pot of salted water on a stove and turn heat on high boil.

2. In a mixing bowl, combine pumpkin, ricotta, flour, egg, nutmeg (if using), salt, and a few grinds of fresh black pepper. Stir gently to form a very soft dough.

3. Dust a clean plate with flour and set it next to your work area. Turn the dough out on a lightly floured surface and divide into six balls. Roll each ball into a long, cylindrical "snake," about ¾-inch thick. Using a very sharp knife, cut into 1-inch "pillows." Set aside on the lightly floured plate.

4. Melt butter in a large frying pan over medium-high heat. Add the onions and sage. Let cook for 6-7 minutes, until onions brown and sage becomes somewhat crispy.

5. While the onions and sage cook, lower the temperature on the boiling water slightly so you have a light boil. Working in batches cook the gnocchi for 2-3 minutes, or until they float to the surface of the pot. Remove with a slotted spoon.

6. Transfer the boiled, drained gnocchi to the butter-onion-sage mixture and toss well to coat all the gnocchi with butter. Let gnocchi cook for 2-2 ½ minutes on each side to ensure they brown nicely.

7. To serve, divide among 2-4 plates and top with more freshly ground black pepper if desired.

8. Serve hot.

vegetable lasagna

At the end of a long, hard day a warm, hearty piece of lasagna can do amazing things for the soul—but who wants to spend 2 hours assembling and baking a lasagna after said long hard day? I present your solution: use fresh potsticker wrappers as an inexpensive and delicious alternative to dry lasagna noodles. Fresh potsticker wrappers are usually found in the supermarket near the tofu. Unlike lasagna noodles, they require no boiling and cook quickly in the oven. When cooked, they taste like fresh pasta yet cost half as much. BrokeAss brilliance.

PREP TIME 0:20 | COOK TIME 0:40

ingredients | Total Cost $14.50

1 cup ricotta | $4

salt and pepper to taste | Pantry

3 tablespoons olive oil | Pantry

1 small zuchinni, sliced into $1/8$-inch thick rounds | $1

1 small eggplant, sliced into $1/8$-inch thick rounds | $1

1 pound package small square potsticker wrappers | $2

4 ounces shredded mozzarella | $4

1 (14 ounce) can simple tomato sauce | $1.50

a few leaves of fresh basil, chopped | $1

directions | Serves 4

1. Preheat oven to 375°F.

2. Mix the ricotta together with a pinch each of the salt and the pepper until evenly distributed.

3. Preheat a pan over high heat. Heat the olive oil. Sprinkle the veggie pieces with salt and cook in pan until soft and browned on both sides. about 3-4 minutes per side.

4. To assemble the lasagna:

5. Line the bottom of an 8 x 8-inch pan. Pyrex or metal baking dish with a couple spoonfuls of the sauce. Lay a single layer of potsticker wrappers over that. Next scatter about a cup of the veggies over top. then an even layer of the ricotta mixture. Repeat layers twice and top it all of with more mozzarella. Add a smattering of the basil leaves.

6. Bake covered with aluminum foil for about 30 minutes. Carefully remove foil and return to the oven for an additional 5 minutes until the cheese is bubbly and lightly browned in spots.

gnocchi with creamy pesto and cherry tomatoes

Toothsome gnocchi is the perfect bed for this creamy pesto. I like to serve it with a big green salad and hot, crusty bread for sopping up the remaining sauce.

PREP TIME 0:05 | COOK TIME 0:05

ingredients | Total Cost $15

1 (12 ounce) package prepared gnocchi (or use Sun Dried Tomato Ricotta Gnocchi, page 118) | $3

$^{1}/_{2}$ cup fresh pesto (page 25) | $8.50 for entire recipe

2 cups cherry tomatoes, halved | $2

$^{1}/_{4}$ cup half-and-half | $1.50 for $^{1}/_{2}$ pint

directions | Serves 2–3

1. Cook gnocchi according to directions in salted water. In a small pot, whisk together pesto and half-and-half over medium heat until well incorporated and hot.

2. Once gnocchi is cooked, toss gently with the creamy pesto and cherry tomatoes. Garnish with leftover pine nuts and Parmesan if desired.

homemade cheese ravioli

Just as in the lasagna recipe, wonton wrappers work overtime by saving you money and giving the appearance of many hours slaved away over a pasta maker, turning out fresh noodles for your dinner companion. For a delicious BrokeAss appetizer, try boiling the raviolis, lightly pan-frying them in olive oil, and serving the marinara on the side as a dipping sauce.

PREP TIME 0:25 | COOK TIME 0:30

ingredients | Total Cost $10.50

1 cup ricotta cheese | $4 for 15 ounces

3 tablespoons grated Parmesan Cheese | $3.50 for 12 ounces

1 handful fresh basil leaves, roughly chopped | $1

3 cloves garlic, minced | Pantry

salt and pepper to taste | Pantry

1 (12 ounce) package square wonton wrappers (about thirty-two wontons) | $2

directions | Serves 2

1. Combine the ricotta, Parmesan, basil, garlic, salt, and pepper. Mix well.

2. To assemble the raviolis, lay one wonton wrapper on a clean, dry surface. Place about one and a half tablespoons filling in the center of the wonton wrapper. Using a pastry brush or a clean finger, wet the edges of the wrapper with water and cover with a second wonton wrapper. Press the edges to seal and transfer to a large plate. Repeat until you have used up all the filling (you should have about sixteen large raviolis).

3. Bring a large pot of salted water to a light boil. Cook 3-4 raviolis at a time just until they float to the surface (should take no more than a minute). Remove with a slotted spoon and transfer to a clean plate. Repeat until all have been cooked.

4. To serve, divide the freshly cooked ravioli between two plates or bowls and top with tomato sauce, pesto, olive oil or butter, more basil, Parmesan, and freshly cracked pepper.

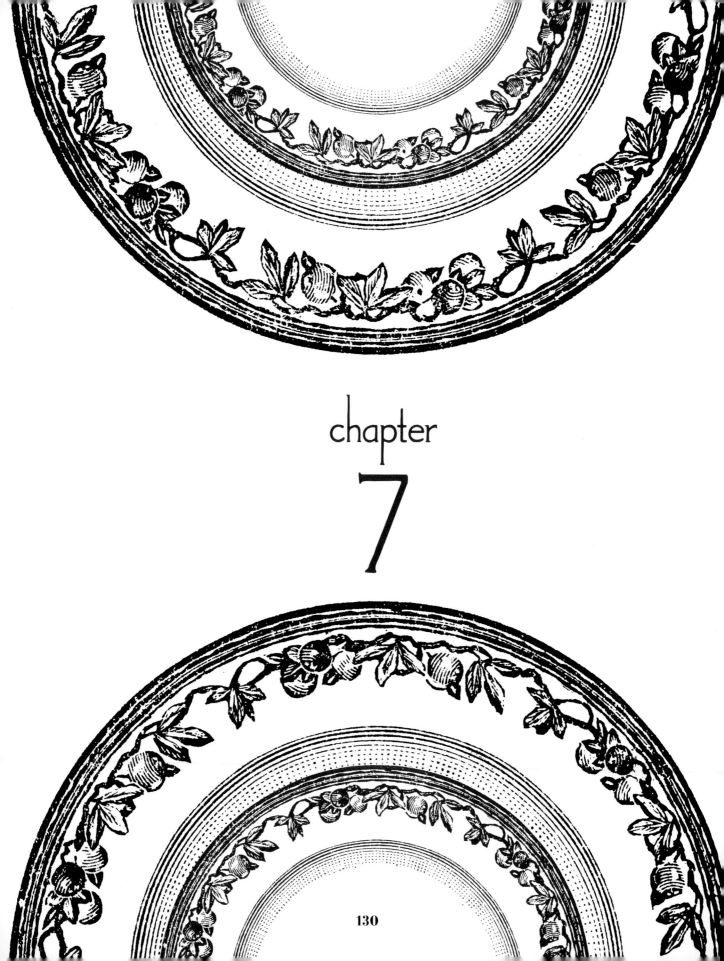

chapter

7

ocean, lake, river, stream

When I was working on this book, I asked my creative friend Andy to help me name this chapter. He emailed me a slew of, um, questionable ideas ("Seafood [not See-Food Like the Kids Show You]," "Swimmers, Sideways Walkers, Filterers and Diggers," "Nemo and Friends," "Stuff That Used to be Really Wet [and Some of Which Still is]") and, finally the title you see above. I liked its simplicity and subtlety, but mostly I liked that it reflected my philosophy when it comes to fish: Keep it basic. Use good, fresh seafood and complement it with clean flavors. Don't overwhelm its delicate flavor with spices and don't try to do too much technique-wise. Seafood is all about paying homage to its origin, so Andy's final title seemed perfect to me.

Remember: Keep it simple, fresh, and reminiscent of its origins and you'll always be golden when it comes to seafood.

roasted salmon with pesto

I invented this one night when it was my turn to host the women in my book club for dinner and literary discussion. We had been reading The Old Man and the Sea, so I wanted to make something oceanic. Roasting the pesto directly on the fish mellows its flavors and draws out the scallions' sugars leaving it almost sweet. I served this over a bed of risotto with seared wax beans, but it hardly needs anything else. Maybe a bit of poached asparagus or a few baby potatoes.

PREP TIME 0:10 | COOK TIME 0:30

ingredients | Total Cost $14

2 (4-ounce) fillets salmon, skin on | $5

Lemon-Scallion pesto | $9

directions | Serves 2

1. Preheat oven to 375°F.

2. Lay the fillets skin-side-down on a baking sheet or in a glass baking dish. Cover completely with a thick layer of the pesto and a slice of lemon and bake for 25-30 minutes or until cooked to desired done-ness.

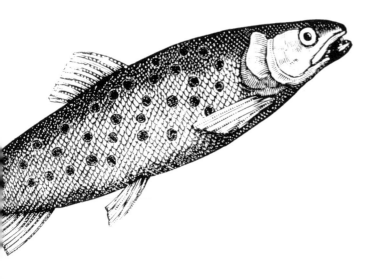

blood orange soy salmon

This salty-sweet rendition of salmon is wonderful served hot alongside rice and vegetables, but I also love it cold over a bed of lightly dressed baby spinach and sliced almonds. Feel free to omit the chili sauce if you're not a fan of spiciness.

PREP TIME 0:25 | COOK TIME 0:12

ingredients | Total Cost $9

2 (4-ounce) fillets of salmon, skin-on | $5

⅛ cup soy sauce | Pantry

2 tablespoons brown sugar | Pantry

2 cloves garlic, minced | Pantry

1 small piece ginger, peeled and minced | $0.50

1 blood orange (half zested and juiced, half sliced into thin rounds) | $0.50

1-2 teaspoon(s) Asian chili sauce (depending on taste) | $2 for 8 ounces

1 small bunch flat-leaf parsley, chopped | $1

directions | Serves 2

1. Preheat oven to 375°F.

2. Combine soy sauce, brown sugar, garlic, ginger, blood orange zest and juice, and chili sauce in a large bowl. Whisk until well-incorporated. Place salmon flesh-side down in the marinade, gently pressing salmon down to ensure that all of it is exposed to the marinade. Allow to marinate like this in the refrigerator for 10 minutes.

3. Once salmon has marinated, place fillets, skin-side down in a glass baking dish. Top each fillet with 1-2 slices of blood orange and bake for 10-12 minutes, or until fish is cooked to desired done-ness.

4. Serve garnished with flat-leaf parsley.

tekka avo maki

If I have one decidedly non-BrokeAss food habit, it's sushi. No doubt about it, fish that is good enough to be served raw will cost you, which is why I was so stoked to find sashimi-grade yellow fin tuna on sale at Safeway, of all places. I added an avocado, some carrots, nori, sesame seeds, and rice to my shopping basket and an hour later I had a yummy sushi dinner for two and plenty of money left over for Sapporo.

Note: If you have a sushi-rolling mat, great, but it's not necessary.

PREP TIME 0:20

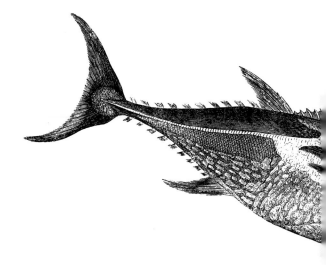

ingredients | Total Cost $16.50

½ pound sashimi grade yellow fin tuna | $6

6 sheets nori | $2.50 for twelve

1 ripe avocado, sliced | $1.50

2 carrots, shredded | $1

1 cup sushi rice, cooked according to package directions and cooled to room temperature | $2.50 for 24 ounces

1 tablespoon rice vinegar | $1.50 for 10 ounces

1 tablespoon sesame seeds | $1.50 for 1 ounce

directions | Makes about thirty pieces of sushi

1. Drizzle the rice vinegar over the rice. Set aside.

2. On a clean surface, slice the tuna into strips about the length and width of your finger (gross, I know). Set aside.

3. Place a sheet of nori, shiny-side-down on a clean cutting board or sushi mat. Wet your hands completely and scoop up a handful of rice. Press an even layer of rice from the bottom of the nori, up about ¾ of the way.

4. Arrange 1 or 2 pieces of tuna, avocado, and some carrot in an even line at the bottom of the nori sheet, on top of the rice layer. Roll the nori tightly, encasing the tuna, avocado, and carrot. Use a little water to seal the end if necessary. If you have a sushi mat, you can use it to roll the sushi at this point. Repeat with remaining nori, rice, tuna, avocado, and carrot.

5. Slice the sushi into 1- or 1 ½-inch pieces. Sprinkle lightly with sesame seeds.

6. Serve garnished with your favorite sushi accompaniments. I prefer lemon, soy sauce, wasabi, and pickled ginger.

baked coconut shrimp

I love crispy fried coconut shrimp, but I don't love how much fat they contain. The baked version of this classic tropical treat is every bit as tasty, but much lighter.

PREP TIME 0:45 | COOK TIME 0:15

ingredients | Total Cost $15

Vegetable oil or cooking spray for greasing baking sheet | Pantry

¼ cup soy sauce | Pantry

2 teaspoons Sriracha or other Asian chili sauce | $2 for 16 ounces

2 teaspoons honey | Pantry

½ teaspoon ground black pepper | Pantry

18-24 medium to large raw shrimp, butterflied (tails can be left on) | $9

2 eggs, beaten | $1.50 for 12

½ cup Japanese panko breadcrumbs | $2.50 for 14 ounces

¼ cup flaked coconut (I used unsweetened, but sweetened would work too) | $2 for 10 ounces

directions | Serves 2–3

1. Preheat oven to 425°F. Lightly grease a baking sheet with the oil or cooking spray and set aside.

2. In a mixing bowl, combine the soy sauce, chili sauce, honey, and black pepper. Stir well. Add the shrimp and toss to combine. Cover with plastic wrap and refrigerate for at least 15 minutes (up to an hour).

3. Mix the panko and coconut together. Toss well.

4. Set up an assembly line in this order: the marinated shrimp, egg, panko-coconut mixture, and prepared baking sheet. Dip a shrimp, holding it by its tail, into the egg, then into the panko-coconut mixture, and place it directly onto the baking sheet. Repeat until all shrimp are coated.

5. Bake the shrimp for about 7 minutes, gently flip and bake for another 7 minutes.

6. Serve the shrimp atop mixed greens as a salad, or as an appetizer with lime wedges, sweet chili sauce or Sriracha for dipping.

italian tuna salad

I have to tell you, I did not expect to like this.

I've always hated regular canned tuna. My mother would stir it into a salad with mayonnaise, chopped celery and onions, with buttery crackers for scooping it up. Many children (and adults) would have loved such a snack. I thought it tasted like cat food . . . not that I knew what cat food tasted like.

Then recently, a friend, whose taste in food I trust, suggested I try Italian-style tuna packed in olive oil. He claimed it was much more delicious than the yucky, water-packed albacore of my youth.

The oil-packed tuna, which I found at Trader Joe's did taste better than I remembered the water-packed kind tasting. Briny, but not fishy, in a delightful way. The fresh, non-creamy additions to the salad made for a light but very filling, protein-packed lunch. Feel free to experiment with different herbs and vegetables.

PREP TIME: 0:15

ingredients | Total Cost $9

1 (5-ounce) can albacore tuna packed in olive oil (do not drain) | $2

¼ medium red onion, sliced very thinly | $0.50 for a whole onion

1 tablespoon capers, drained | $2 for a 4-ounce jar

about 10 cherry or grape tomatoes, halved | $3.50 for a pint

1 small handful fresh flat-leaf parsley leaves, chopped | $1 for a bunch

1 teaspoon balsamic vinegar | Pantry

salt and freshly ground black pepper to taste | Pantry

directions | Serves 1–2

1. Place the tuna and all of its oil into a mixing bowl. Use a fork to gently flake the tuna. Combine all other ingredients, toss gently, and serve immediately.

JUST LIKE MOM USED TO MAKE . . .
IF YOUR MOM WAS A CLASSY
ITALIAN CHEF.

crab cakes with lemon-caper mayonnaise

I've spent many a sunny weekend afternoon drinking beer and eating crispy crab cakes waterside at Sam's Anchor Cafe in Tiburon, CA. This recipe is a (way) less expensive version of Sam's delicious crab cakes and can be procured without the ferry ride (or the sunburn).

PREP TIME 0:20 | COOK TIME 0:05

ingredients | Total Cost $12

2 (6-ounce) cans crab meat (I prefer Trader Joe's 15 percent leg meat), drained | $3.50

$1/2$ small white onion, finely chopped | $0.50

1 small bunch parsley, plus more for garnish, chopped | $1

$1/3$ cup bread crumbs | $2 for 16 ounces

7 tablespoons mayonnaise, divided | Pantry

1 egg, lightly beaten | $1.50 for 6

1 pinch each salt and pepper | Pantry

1 lemon, half juiced, half cut into wedges | $0.50

1 tablespoon capers, finely chopped | $3 for a 4-ounce jar

1 clove garlic, finely minced | Pantry

olive oil for frying | Pantry

directions | Makes 8–10 small crab cakes

1. Combine crab, onion, parsley, bread crumbs, 2 tablespoons mayonnaise, egg, salt, and pepper in a mixing bowl. Gently combine until ingredients come together. If mixture is too wet, add a little more breadcrumbs. Likewise, if it is too dry, add slightly more mayonnaise.

2. Use wet hands to form mixture into eight to ten 3-inch patties. Set on a clean plate.

3. Pour about $\frac{1}{4}$ of olive oil into a large frying pan and heat over medium-high heat. Cook crab cakes, a few at a time for 2½-3 minutes or until golden-brown and crispy. Use a spatula to carefully flip the cakes and cook until brown and crispy on the other side. Drain on paper towels. Repeat until all crab cakes are cooked.

4. To make the lemon-caper mayonnaise, whisk together the remaining mayonnaise, lemon juice, capers, and garlic. Add a pinch of pepper if desired. Serve alongside crab cakes for dipping.

shrimp with spicy pesto and mango

I lose my appetite when it gets hot. I go about my day, soaking up the sunshine and sipping iced coffee and then, before I know it, it's 4 P.M. and I'm starving and way too weak and overheated to turn the oven on.

Enter this easy, fresh, and light dinner. Ready in 20 minutes, healthy and full of great flavors and textures. Serve it with rice or noodles if you want but it's lovely on its own.

PREP TIME 0:15 | COOK TIME 0:05

ingredients | Total Cost $11.75

1 handful fresh cilantro leaves | $1 for a bunch

1 handful fresh, flat-leaf parsley leaves | $1 for a bunch

1 handful fresh mint leaves | $1 for a bunch

$\frac{1}{2}$ green jalapeño, seeded and chopped | $0.25

2 cloves garlic, peeled and smashed | Pantry

juice of 2 lime, divided | $1

3 tablespoons extra virgin olive oil, divided | Pantry

salt and pepper to taste | Pantry

$\frac{1}{2}$ pound peeled, de-veined medium shrimp | $5

1 tablespoon soy sauce | Pantry

$\frac{1}{2}$ mango, diced | $1

$\frac{1}{2}$ cucumber, peeled and diced | $0.50

$\frac{1}{2}$ red bell pepper, seeded and diced | $1

directions | Serves 2

1. Combine cilantro, parsley, mint, jalapeño, garlic, juice of 1 lime and 2 tablespoons olive oil in a food processor or blender. Pulse until smooth. Season with salt and pepper to taste. Set aside.

2. Sprinkle shrimp with soy sauce. Toss to coat.

3. Heat remaining olive oil in a medium frying pan over medium-high heat. Add shrimp and cook, stirring occasionally, until just pink and firm, about 5 minutes. Remove from heat.

4. Toss shrimp with pesto mixture and transfer to serving platter or individual plates.

5. In a medium bowl, combine mango, cucumber, red bell pepper, remaining lime juice, salt, and pepper to taste. Mix until well combined.

6. Top shrimp with mango mixture.

7. Serve immediately, or chill and serve cold.

THESE WILL HAVE YOUR GUESTS

FIGHTING OVER CRUMBS.

LITERALLY.

panko shrimp cakes

I made these for my friend Andrew on a random weeknight about three years ago and he still talks about them. They're basically a more filling, cheaper version of crab cakes. Serve them on their own or over lightly dressed greens.

PREP TIME 0:20 | COOK TIME 0:06

ingredients | Total Cost $13

²/₃ pound de-veined medium raw shrimp, tails removed, chopped medium-finely | $6.50

¹/₂ cup mayonnaise (divided) | Pantry

2 scallions (green onions), sliced | $1 for a bunch

juice of ¹/₂ lemon | $0.50 for a whole lemon

Sriracha or other Asian chili sauce | $2 for 8 ounces

1 small handful fresh cilantro, finely chopped | $1 for a bunch

¹/₄ teaspoon salt | Pantry

few grinds of black pepper | Pantry

1¹/₂ cups Panko bread crumbs | $3 for 16 ounces

2 tablespoons (plus more as needed) vegetable or canola oil, for frying | Pantry

directions | Serves 2–3

1. Combine shrimp, ¹/₄ cup mayonnaise, scallions, lemon juice, 2 teaspoons Sriracha or other chili sauce, cilantro, salt, pepper, and Panko together in a mixing bowl. Form into seven to eight 3-inch patties and set onto a clean plate or cutting board.

2. Heat the oil in a large nonstick frying pan over medium-high heat. Fry the shrimp cakes for 2-3 minutes on each side, until golden-brown and crispy. Drain on paper towels.

3. To make the aioli, simply mix the remaining ¹/₄ cup mayonnaise with 2-3 teaspoons (or more/less to taste—I like about 4 teaspoons) Sriracha/chili sauce.

4. Serve the warm shrimp cakes with the aioli.

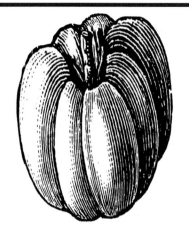

shrimp fajitas

I know those handy-dandy spice fajita seasoning packets seem like a great deal, but don't bother. First of all, they're full of far more sodium than you'd ever actually want to eat. Secondly, for a one-time purchase of a little chili powder and cumin you can make fajitas over and over again. I like to switch up the protein—chicken, skirt steak, and even tempeh are all great choices.

PREP TIME 0:15 | COOK TIME 0:15

ingredients | Total Cost $16.50

8 fajita-sized flour tortillas | $1.50

1 tablespoon vegetable oil | Pantry

$\frac{1}{2}$ yellow onion, cut into 1-inch chunks | $1

1 red bell pepper, seeded and cut into 1-inch strips | $0.50

1 green bell pepper, seeded and cut into 1-inch strips | $0.50

1 cup broccoli florets | $1

1 cup button mushrooms, sliced | $1

2 cloves garlic, minced | Pantry

2 teaspoons cumin | $1.50 for 1 ounce

2 teaspoons chili powder | $1.50 for 1 ounce

1 teaspoon salt | Pantry

2 teaspoons freshly ground pepper | Pantry

$\frac{1}{2}$ pound medium shrimp, tails removed | $8

directions | Serves 4

1. Preheat the oven to 300°F. Wrap the tortillas tightly in foil and place in the warm oven.

2. Heat the oil in a large cast-iron skillet (or other heavy skillet) over high heat. Add the onion and cook for 1 minute. Add the peppers, broccoli, mushrooms, and garlic and cook for another 2 minutes until the onions begin soften.

3. While the vegetables cook, combine the cumin, chili powder, salt, and pepper in a small bowl and whisk together with $\frac{1}{4}$ cup water. Set aside.

4. Add the shrimp to the fajita pan and pour the spice mixture over the entire contents of the pan. Cook just until the shrimp turn pink.

5. Pull the tortillas out of the oven, take them out of the foil and wrap in a clean dish towel or napkin. Serve the fajitas in the pan so they stay warm and wrap the vegetable-shrimp mixture in hot tortillas at the table. Also delicious with guacamole or sour cream.

sole with goat cheese, chives, and lemon

This dish takes 20 minutes to throw together, but is full of sophistication. The long chives are a dramatic touch, making this dish a nice alternative to plain baked fish. Sole is delicate yet buttery, so rich flavors of goat cheese and olive oil work nicely with it while the lemon and chives add nice freshness.

PREP TIME 0:10 | COOK TIME 0:12

ingredients | Total Cost $9

6 ounces soft goat cheese | $3.50 for 8 ounces

2 cloves garlic, minced | Pantry

1 lemon—half juiced, half sliced into 4 thin rounds | $0.50

2 tablespoons extra virgin olive oil plus more for the pan | Pantry

salt and pepper to taste | Pantry

4 fillets (about ¼ lb each) Dover sole | $4

1 bunch fresh chives | $1

directions | Serves 4

1. Preheat oven to 375°F. Lightly oil a baking sheet and set aside.

2. Use the back of a fork to mash the goat cheese with the garlic, lemon juice, olive oil, salt, and pepper.

3. Lay a sole fillet on a clean cutting board and use a butter knife or rubber spatula to spread it liberally with ¼ of the goat cheese mixture. Lay a small bunch of chives (7-8 long ones) in the center of the cheese, so that the fish and the chives form a cross.

4. Gently roll the sole around the chives, cheese-side in, so the chives are sticking out of either end of the wrapped-up fish. Place on the prepared pan. Repeat with remaining fish, filling, and chives.

5. Top each sole roll-up with a slice of lemon and gently secure with a toothpick. Top with more pepper and bake for 10-12 minutes (check after 8 minutes to avoid over-cooking). The fish is done when it's tender but cooked-through and the cheese is warm and very soft.

6. Serve immediately.

HEART AND SOLE,

I FELL IN LOVE

WITH YOU . . .

lemon-scallop rice cakes with tangy yogurt sauce

When you think of rice cakes, you likely think of the Styrofoam-like disks that are so wonderful for holding a smear of peanut butter, jelly, or hummus. But the lunchtime staple made so popular in the 1970s is entirely different from this dish, which showcases chewy short-grain rice and fresh scallops. While scallops are usually an expensive treat, this dish is a great way to stretch their fresh taste and lovely texture. The bright flavors of lemon and parsley go a long way to make this dish light yet satisfying.

PREP TIME 0:15 | COOK TIME 0:08

ingredients | Total Cost $12

1 cup short grain rice | $1

$1/4$ pound large sea scallops | $6

1 small bunch parsley, finely chopped | $1

zest and juice of one lemon | $0.50

4 scallions, sliced | $1

$1/2$ small white onion, minced | $1

$1/2$ cup Greek yogurt | $1.50

2 tablespoons extra virgin olive oil | Pantry

salt and pepper to taste | Pantry

directions | Serves 2

1. Cook the rice according to directions. Transfer into a medium bowl and allow to cool.

2. Chop the scallops into $1/2$-inch pieces. Combine the scallops, parsley scallions, lemon zest, onion, and a pinch each of salt and pepper with the cooled, cooked rice until well-incorporated.

3. Wet your hands with water (to prevent sticking) and form the mixture into six 3-4-inch patties. Set on a clean plate or cutting board.

4. Heat the olive oil in a large frying pan over medium-high heat. Fry the patties for 3-4 minutes on each side, allowing a crisp, golden-brown crust to develop on both sides. Divide the patties between two plates.

5. Whisk together the yogurt, lemon juice, salt, and pepper to taste. Drizzle over the top of the patties. Garnish with additional lemon and parsley if desired.

YOU'RE A PO BOY
(OR GIRL). OWN IT!

cornmeal shrimp po boy

I figured I really couldn't write a book about cheap food without including the Louisiana classic po' boy sandwich. Though these ingredients make just two sandwiches, if you can part with just a few more bucks for a full pound of shrimp, you can easily feed four with the ingredients below.

I also like spicing up the mayonnaise with a bit of Sriracha.

PREP TIME 0:15 | COOK TIME 0:05

ingredients | Total Cost $12.50

canola or vegetable oil, for frying | Pantry

2/3 cup medium-grind cornmeal | $2 for 14 ounces

1/2 pound raw medium shrimp, peeled, deveined, tails removed | $6.50

salt and pepper to taste | Pantry

1/2 baguette, sliced lengthwise and into two 6-inch lengths (for two sandwiches) | $2 for a whole baguette

4 tablespoons mayonnaise | Pantry

1/2 ripe tomato, sliced | $0.50 for a whole tomato

2 pickles, sliced | $2 for a 12-ounce jar

3-4 Romaine lettuce leaves, torn | $1.50 for a head

directions | Serves 2

1. Heat about 1 inch of oil in a large frying pan over medium-high heat, until a drop of water sizzles when dropped in.

2. Place the cornmeal in a bowl and set it and the shrimp next to the stove. Dredge the shrimp, a few at a time, in the cornmeal, making sure they are completely covered, then drop into the hot oil. Cook for 1-2 minutes on each side, until the shrimp curl up and are golden-brown on the outside.

3. Drain the cooked shrimp on paper towels and sprinkle immediately with salt and pepper.

4. To assemble the sandwiches, spread the bread with the mayonnaise and layer with the cooked shrimp, tomato, pickles, Romaine, and more salt and pepper to taste if desired.

chapter

8

bet the farm

For nearly twenty years, I was a vegetarian. Thanks to a long afternoon spent at the petting zoo at my hometown's county fair when I was in the second grade, I spent the bulk of my youth and early adulthood eschewing meat and poultry (I had an off-again-on-again relationship with eggs, fish, and dairy). One day, when I was twenty-seven, I decided that perhaps it had been long enough and maybe I should give meat a try again. I started with plain, poached chicken and slowly worked my way up the food (and flavor) chain. Today, I eat everything and am so happy I do. Meat isn't for everyone, but if it's for you, you'll do well to learn a few simple techniques for turning inexpensive pieces of meat into gourmet masterpieces.

When I can afford to, I prefer to buy grass-fed meats and free-range, hormone-free poultry. Trader Joe's usually offers good deals on these items.

mexican sausage patties

Once you try making your own breakfast sausage patties, you'll never go back to the preservative-laden commercial variety. I happened to have ingredients for Mexican sausages on hand, but feel free to get creative. The only requirements are ground pork (or turkey), garlic, onion, salt, pepper, and brown sugar.

PREP TIME 0:15 | COOK TIME 0:10

ingredients | Total Cost $5.25

1 pound ground pork | $2

1 green jalapeño, finely diced | $0.25

2 cloves garlic, chopped | Pantry

1/2 small onion, minced | $0.50

1 handful fresh cilantro, finely chopped | $1 for a bunch

1 teaspoon ground cumin | $1.50 for 1 ounce

1 teaspoon each salt and pepper | Pantry

2 tablespoons brown sugar | Pantry

1 tablespoon olive, vegetable or canola oil for frying | Pantry

directions | Serves 4–6

1. Combine all ingredients except oil in a mixing bowl. Use your hands to combine well and form into 2-inch sausage patties.

2. Heat oil in a medium frying pan over medium-high heat and, working in batches, cook sausages for 2-3 minutes on each side, or until brown on the outside and cooked through on the inside.

3. Serve immediately.

kielbasa with apples and onions

This is my favorite way to serve sausages. The apples caramelize slightly when grilled and the amazing taste of lightly charred onions is outstanding. This dish is even more awesome prepared on an outside charcoal or gas grill.

PREP TIME 0:05 | COOK TIME 0:10

ingredients | Total Cost $7.50

2 tablespoons olive oil | Pantry

1 white onion, sliced into rings | $0.50

2 tart apples, thinly sliced | $1

2 kielbasa sausages, sliced on the diagonal | $6

salt and pepper to taste | Pantry

directions | Serves 2–4

1. Heat olive oil in a large grill pan or cast-iron pan over high heat. Grill onion, apples, and sausage slices in batches on both sides.

2. Season with salt and pepper.

seared steak with red wine sauce and broccolini

Flank steak is one of the most BrokeAss-friendly cuts of meat available. It's rich and flavorful on its own but also takes well to whatever you put on it and, most important, it tastes delicious without breaking the bank. The luxurious wine sauce will make you feel as if you are eating in a fancy restaurant and the lemony broccolini (which is milder-tasting and thinner than broccoli but equally full of antioxidants) is the perfect accompaniment.

PREP TIME 1:15 | COOK TIME 1:15

ingredients | Total Cost $13

1 (8-ounce) flank steak | $4

Soy sauce | Pantry

salt and pepper | Pantry

Leaves of 1 fresh thyme sprig | $1

6 green onions, sliced | $1

1/2 bottle red inexpensive red wine | $2.50 for a bottle

1 stick unsalted butter | $1.50

1 small bunch flat leaf parsley, chopped | $1

directions | Serves 2

1. Place steak on a large plate or in a baking dish and brush with soy sauce. Add thyme and sprinkle lightly with salt and pepper to taste. Let stand for 1 hour. Brush again with soy sauce and place on a hot grill pan or barbeque over high heat for 1-2 minutes on each side for rare steak (3-4 minutes on each side for medium, 4-5 minutes on each side for well-done). Slice steak on the diagonal.

2. To make the sauce, combine green onions and wine in a medium saucepan and bring to a light boil. Add butter and parsley and allow to cook for another 2-3 minutes. Slice the steak on the diagonal and arrange prettily on plates. Spoon sauce over steak and serve with the broccolini.

ingredients | Total Cost $3.50

1 pound broccolini, or use regular broccoli | $3

salt and pepper to taste | Pantry

1 tablespoon olive oil | Pantry

2 cloves garlic, minced | Pantry

1 lemon, 1/2 juiced, other 1/2 cut into wedges. | $0.50

directions

1. Trim ends off broccolini. Place the broccolini in a large frying pan and cover with water. Cover pan and bring to a boil. Simmer broccolini 6-7 minutes, until tender and bright green. Drain the broccolini and set aside. Heat the olive oil in pan over medium heat and add the garlic. Cook garlic 1-2 minutes and return broccolini to the pan. Add lemon juice and salt and pepper to the broccolini and toss well to ensure that each piece is well-coated.

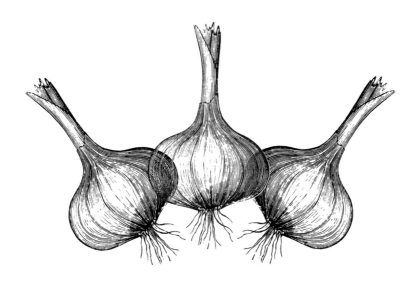

balsamic-glazed rib eye with seared tomatoes

This easy rib eye recipe is unbelievably quick to throw together and its magical marinade would be great on chicken, too. If you have it, try subbing maple syrup for the brown sugar for a slightly different but equally delicious touch of sweetness.

PREP TIME 0:40 (including marinating) | COOK TIME 0:10

ingredients | Total Cost $10

3 tablespoons balsamic vinegar | Pantry

1½ tablespoons brown sugar | Pantry

2 tablespoons soy sauce | Pantry

salt and pepper to taste | Pantry

1 (14-16 ounce) rib eye steak, fat trimmed | $6

extra virgin olive oil for brushing grill | Pantry

10 cherry tomatoes, halved | $3 for a pint

1 handful fresh basil leaves, chopped | $1

directions | Serves 2

1. Whisk together the balsamic vinegar, brown sugar, soy sauce, salt, and pepper to taste. Pour into an airtight container or zip-top plastic bag. Place steak in container or bag, making sure it is completely immersed in liquid. Seal/cover and marinate in refrigerator for at least 30 minutes or as long as overnight.

2. Heat a grill or grill pan over high heat and brush with olive oil (if using an indoor grill or grill pan). Cook steak to desired done-ness on both sides.

3. While steak cooks, sear tomatoes for 1 minute on each side. This can be done in the same grill pan as you cook the steak, if using. Otherwise, use a small skillet on cooktop or outside grill and brush lightly with olive oil. Remove the seared tomatoes from the heat and toss gently with the chopped basil and a little salt and pepper.

4. To serve the steak, slice on the bias and arrange. Top with tomato mixture.

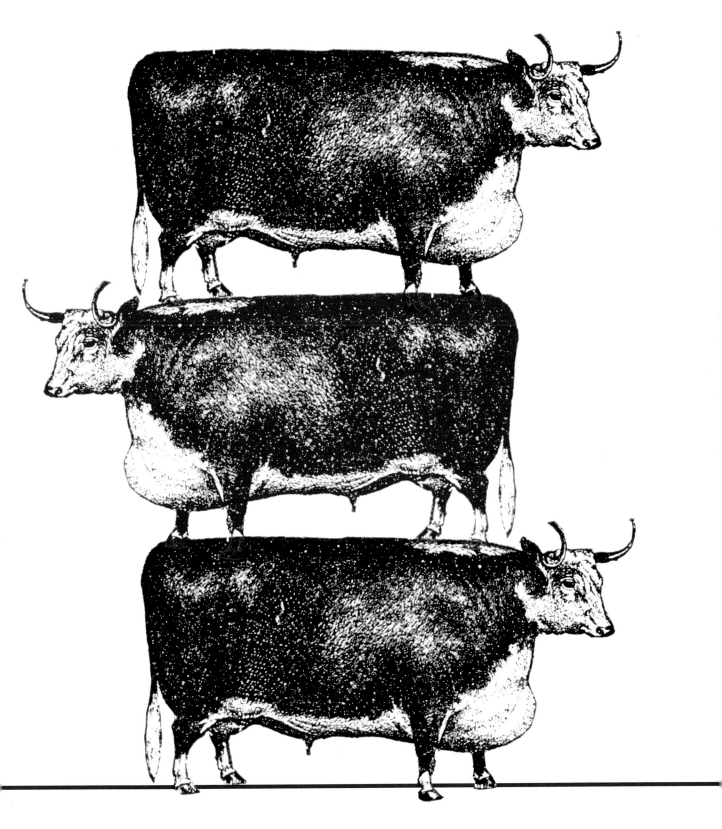

grilled lamb chops over carrot-gorgonzola smash

I made these one night at a friend's house. He was craving mashed potatoes to go along with the lamb chops I was making, and, having no potatoes to peel, boil, and mash, I went with carrots instead. The sweet, rich mixture that resulted benefitted gloriously from a touch of creamy, pungent gorgonzola, making the perfect bed for the oil-and-herb-marinated lamb chops.

Note: Have your butcher cut the lamb chops into individual "lollipops" for you.

PREP TIME 0:45 | COOK TIME 0:25

162

ingredients | Total Cost $20

5 tablespoons olive oil, divided | Pantry

3 cloves garlic, minced | Pantry

1 small bunch flat leaf parsley, finely chopped | $1

salt and pepper to taste | Pantry

6 fresh lamb chops, bone-in | $13

8 carrots, peeled and chopped | $2

1 ounce gorgonzola dolce, crumbled | $4

directions | Serves 6

1. Combine 3 tablespoons olive oil, garlic, parsley, salt, and pepper in a large bowl. Add lamb chops and toss to coat. Cover tightly with saran wrap and refrigerate for 30 minutes.

2. While lamb marinates, make the smash. Boil carrots in hot, salted water for 20-25 minutes or until very soft. Drain and return to pot. Mash in remaining olive oil and gorgonzola. Season with salt and pepper to taste. Smash using the back of a fork until very creamy with few chunks.

3. When lamb has finished marinating, remove from refrigerator, uncover, and bring to room temperature, about 10 minutes.

4. Heat a grill pan or regular grill to high heat. Grill lamb chops for 4-5 minutes on each side, depending on desired doneness. To serve, spoon a bit of the carrot smash onto a plate and top each pile of smash with a lamb chop. Garnish with more parsley if desired.

pan-braised chipotle short ribs

If time management in the kitchen is a problem for you, look no further than this recipe. These short ribs take only a few minutes to throw together before braising for 2 hours, leaving you plenty of time to throw together some potato salad or coleslaw and maybe even throw together a simple dessert.

Note: Save any leftover sauce to brush over chicken or burgers the next time you grill. It'll keep in an airtight container in the fridge for about a week.

PREP TIME 0:20 | COOK TIME 2:00

ingredients | Total Cost $13.50

2 pounds beef short ribs | $10

2 tablespoons olive or vegetable oil | Pantry

1 (14.5-ounce) can fire-roasted crushed tomatoes | $2

1 (7-ounce) can chipotle chilies canned in adobo, plus the sauce from the can | $1.50

2 tablespoons brown sugar | Pantry

3 cloves garlic, smashed | Pantry

salt and pepper | Pantry

directions | Serves 2

1. Pat the short ribs dry with a paper towel. Season lightly with salt and pepper.

2. Heat oil in a deep, large frying pan (make sure it has a fitted lid for use later in the recipe) over high heat. Brown the fleshy side of the short ribs in the oil, 2-3 minutes.

3. While short ribs brown, combine crushed tomatoes (reserve the can), chipotle chilies and sauce, brown sugar, garlic, and salt and pepper to taste in a blender. Puree until smooth. Pour mixture over short ribs in pan, making sure the short ribs are fleshy-side down in the sauce. Fill the crushed tomatoes can with water and pour over the ribs. Cover pan with lid and reduce heat to medium.

4. Cook, covered for 2 hours, or until beef is very tender.

5. Serve hot with a few spoonfuls of sauce.

HOT, SPICY AND MELTINGLY

TENDER . . . JUST LIKE YOU.

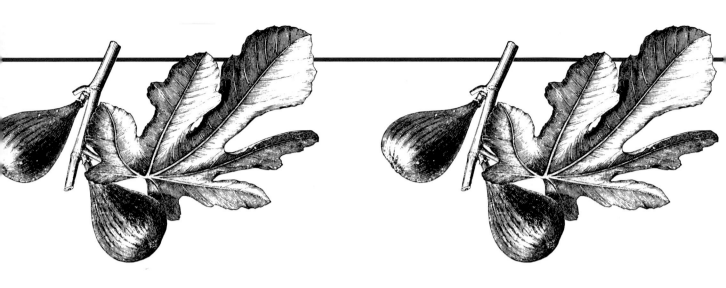

rosemary-shallot pork tenderloin with fig compote

My friend, Paul, likes to tease me about my tendency to combine sweet and savory flavor elements in recipes. I pretend to be annoyed, but all things considered, it's pretty generous of him considering he knows me well enough to come up with measurably worse things to rib me about. So go to town Paul—I'm ready for your running commentary. When fig season arrives, I just can't resist this dish.

PREP TIME 0:30 | COOK TIME 0:28

ingredients | Total Cost $7.25

1 shallot, diced | $0.25

3 cloves garlic, chopped | Pantry

2 tablespoons olive oil, plus more for pan | Pantry

leaves from 2 springs of fresh rosemary, chopped | $1

salt and pepper to taste | Pantry

1 pound pork tenderloin | $3

8 fresh figs (any kind), stems removed, diced | $3 for a carton

¼ cup balsamic vinegar | Pantry

1 tablespoon honey | Pantry

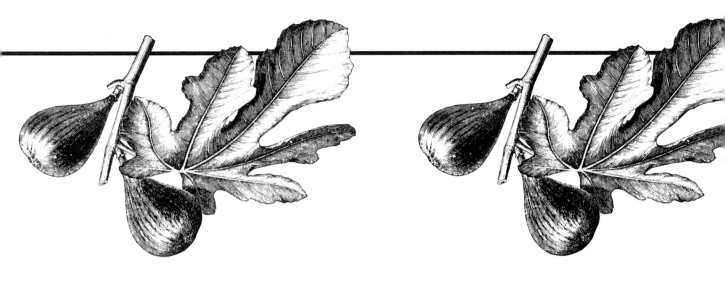

directions | Serves 3–4

1. Preheat oven to 400°F. Lightly oil a baking dish and set aside.

2. Combine shallot, garlic, olive oil, rosemary, salt, and pepper to taste in a small bowl. Set aside.

3. Using a sharp knife, butterfly the tenderloin by making a horizontal slice lengthwise through the tenderloin almost all the way to the other side. Open the meat like a book. Cover with plastic wrap, and use a meat mallet, rolling pin, or small cast-iron skillet to pound the pork so that it's about $1/2$ thick.

4. Pour shallot-garlic mixture over one lengthwise side of the pork and roll up, securing tightly with toothpicks or cooking twine.

5. Roast in oven for 22–28 minutes or until pork is cooked thoroughly and very fragrant.

6. While pork cooks, combine figs, balsamic vinegar, honey, salt, and pepper to taste in a small pot over medium-high heat. Cook until reduced to a thick jamlike consistency. Turn off heat.

7. To serve, slice pork into 4 to 6 slices. Serve pork slices topped with a few spoonfuls of compote and more fresh rosemary for garnish.

chinese pork meatballs with sweetpotatoes and peanut sauce

Truth be told, I invented this recipe when I was trying to impress a guy I was dating who, mentioned, during two separate dates and thus, two separate conversations, that he loved both meatballs and peanut sauce. My plot to win his heart failed, but it did leave with this fantastic dish. You can use ground turkey or chicken in place of the pork, but the meatballs won't be as juicy as flavorful as when pork is used.

PREP TIME 0:25 | COOK TIME 0:18

ingredients | Total Cost $11.50

1 pound ground pork (feel free to use ground turkey or chicken if you prefer) | $2

1 (1 inch) piece ginger, peeled and chopped | $0.50

2 cloves garlic, chopped | Pantry

2 scallions, chopped | $1 for a bunch

1/2 small onion, finely diced | $0.50

2 teaspoons soy sauce | Pantry

1-2 teaspoons (more/less to taste) Asian chili sauce | price included in cost of peanut sauce ingredients

1 medium garnet yam, scrubbed and diced | $0.50

salt to taste | Pantry

1/2 cup peanut sauce (see recipe, page 19) | $7

1 handful fresh cilantro leaves, chopped | price included in cost of peanut sauce ingredients

directions | Serves 2–4

1. Preheat oven to 375°F. Lightly grease a baking sheet and set aside.

2. In a mixing bowl, combine pork, ginger, garlic, scallions, onion, soy sauce, and chili sauce. Use hands to mix well. Form into golf ball-sized balls and place on one half of the prepared baking sheet.

3. Spread the diced sweet potato evenly on the other half of the baking sheet. Sprinkle lightly with salt.

4. Bake for 10-12 minutes, or until the meatballs are cooked through but still juicy. Leave the oven on.

5. Pour the peanut sauce into the bottom of a large pie/casserole dish, cast-iron or other oven-proof skillet. Arrange the meatballs evenly in the sauce and scatter the sweet potatoes around the meatballs. Return to the oven and cook for 4-5 minutes, or until peanut sauce is heated.

6. Top with a shower of chopped cilantro and serve immediately.

third-date chicken

I rarely cook on first, or even second dates. I know it seems like it should be my go-to activity (an opportunity to tantalize the taste buds of my potential paramour!), but it gets weird when cooking is your job. First of all, the pressure's on to impress (as if it weren't already anyway) and it requires me to try to look cute while chopping onions (just try it). Moreover, it feels akin to asking a dentist out and then asking him to take a quick peek at your molars.

That said, by date number three, I am usually comfortable enough to invite a man into my kitchen, and this is my trusty stand-by meal, assuming he eats poultry (I do live in San Francisco, so the possibility that he is a raw foodist gluten-free vegan is not out of the realm of possibility). I get the chicken prepped and into the oven before he shows up (which has the side benefit of making my apartment smell amazing), roast some sweet potatoes or whip up some risotto and throw together a green salad.

Even if you aren't planning a hot date any time soon, this chicken is great to make on a Sunday, and then eat throughout the week. I tuck pieces of it into sandwiches, wrap it in burritos or pack it cold to take on a picnic.

PREP TIME 0:15 | COOK TIME 1:05

ingredients | Total Cost $9.50

1 whole (4-5 pound) roasting chicken, giblets removed | $8

$^1/_2$ cup extra virgin olive oil | Pantry

12 garlic cloves, chopped | Pantry

leaves from 2 sprigs fresh rosemary | $1 for a bunch

1 lemon, zested and thinly sliced | $0.50

2 teaspoons each salt and pepper | Pantry

directions | Serves 4–6

1. Preheat oven to 375°F.

2. Rinse the chicken under cool running water and pat dry, using paper towels. Place in a large (at least 9 x 13-inch) casserole pan.

3. Whisk together the olive oil, garlic, rosemary, lemon zest, salt, and pepper (you can also leave the garlic cloves whole and blend it all together in a food processor or blender).

4. Pour a bit of the oil-garlic mixture into the cupped palm of your hand and rub it over the skin of the chicken on both sides. Gently slide your hands between the skin and the flesh of the chicken and rub some of the oil mixture beneath the skin. Pour a bit more oil into your hands and rub the cavity of the chicken with it. Continue until the whole chicken is covered with the garlic-oil mixture.

5. Place a few slices of lemon between the skin and the flesh. Stuff the rest of the slices into the cavity. Arrange chicken breast side up in the pan and use kitchen twine or a couple of toothpicks to attach the legs together. Cover the pan tightly with aluminum foil.

6. Bake, covered, for 30 minutes. Remove the foil and bake, uncovered, for another 25-30 minutes, or until the skin is golden-brown and the juices run clear (stab a knife into the thigh to check this).

7. Cut into pieces and serve hot.

8. If you want to make pan gravy, pour the pan juices (there should be plenty) into a small pot over high and bring to a light boil. Sprinkle in 1-2 tablespoons of flour and whisk constantly (breaking up the lumps) until a thick, creamy gravy forms. Serve alongside the chicken.

cilantro pesto-stuffed chicken breasts over pinto beans

Stuffed chicken breasts are a great way to make your dinner look really fancy without a lot of effort. Plus, after a long day there are few things more satisfying than pounding raw chicken with a mallet.

Lentils or black beans would also be good as a base for the chicken.

PREP TIME 0:20 | COOK TIME 0:25

ingredients | Total Cost $16

extra virgin olive oil | Pantry

2 boneless, skinless chicken breasts | $7

1 small bunch cilantro plus extra for garnish | $2

3 cloves garlic, peeled | Pantry

juice and zest of ½ lemon | $0.50

¼ cup shredded mozzarella cheese | $3.50 for 8 oz.

salt and pepper to taste | Pantry

1 (15-ounce) can refried or whole pinto beans | $1.50

3 tablespoons water

directions | Serves 2

1. Preheat oven to 375°F. Use 1 teaspoon olive oil to lightly grease a baking dish.

2. Place a chicken breast between two pieces of wax paper and pound to $\frac{1}{4}$-inch thickness using a mallet or a rolling pin. Repeat with second breast.

3. In a food processor or blender, combine cilantro, garlic, 3 tablespoons olive oil, lemon juice and zest, and mozzarella until a chunky paste forms. Season with salt and pepper to taste.

4. To assemble chicken, spread half of the pesto over the top of a chicken breast. Roll up tightly to form a cylinder and secure using toothpicks. Repeat with second chicken breast and remaining pesto. Place in prepared baking dish.

5. Bake for 20-25 minutes or until just cooked. Test the chicken by cutting a slice to see if the chicken has cooked all the way through before serving.

6. While chicken bakes, drain the beans and heat in a small pot over medium-high heat with 3 tablespoons water until hot. Mash with a fork until mostly smooth. Season lightly with salt.

7. To serve, divide portions of the beans onto two plates. Cut chicken into 1-inch pinwheel slices and serve over beans. Garnish with additional cilantro.

I'M PRETTY SURE THE CHICKEN WOULDN'T HAVE CROSSED THE ROAD IF HE KNEW THIS WOULD BE THE RESULT.

roasted hot-sauce chicken

The brilliance of this recipe lies in the effect that slow-roasting has on most hot sauces. After spending a long time in the oven at a relatively low temperature, your formerly spicy hot sauce mellows out, making it a suitable coating for a tender chicken. This is a good one to make on Sunday evening and eat throughout the week.

Note: Thick, pastelike hot sauces work best in this recipe (see suggestions below).

PREP TIME 0:25 | COOK TIME 1:15

ingredients | Total Cost $11–$13

1 (4-4½ pound) roasting chicken, giblets removed | $8

salt and pepper | Pantry

6 tablespoons thick hot sauce (suggestions: harissa, sambal or Sriracha) approx. | $2.50–$4.50 for a jar/bottle

extra-virgin olive for brushing | Pantry

1 lemon, cut into wedges, for serving | Pantry

directions | Serves 3–4

1. Preheat oven to 325°F.

2. Rinse chicken cavity and exterior under cool running water. Use paper towels to pat it dry. Sprinkle salt and pepper liberally all over chicken. Place chicken breast up in an 11 x 13-inch casserole or roasting pan.

3. Working in 1-tablespoon increments, rub the hot sauce all over the chicken, outside and inside. Use your hands to gently loosen the chicken skin and rub some sauce in between the chicken's skin and its flesh. Make sure the whole thing is well-covered. Set chicken in pan aside and wash hands thoroughly. Cover pan tightly with aluminum foil.

4. Roast for 45 minutes with foil on. Uncover and brush top of chicken lightly with olive oil (this helps the skin retain moisture) and roast, uncovered for another 25-30 minutes. Chicken is done when juices from a pierced thigh run clear.

5. Serve with lemons for squeezing and a shower of fresh chopped cilantro or flat-leaf parsley.

sweet potato-chicken mole

My parents love to tell a story wherein I, at age fourteen months, was given a bite of spicy Mexican mole (kind of shoddy parenting there, if you ask me, mom and dad!) and did a dance known as "the chicken," shrieking at the top of my lungs, due to the excruciating pain my sensitive baby tongue was experiencing.

Anyway, childhood anecdotes aside, this delicious, easy mole dish is perfect for a crowd, as it serves up to six people, but it is also a great dish to cook on Sunday night and eat for the rest of the week. The first night I make it, I serve it with steamed rice on the side, and then with warm corn tortillas, chopped onions, cilantro, and Mexican crema for all the days thereafter. Vegetarians should use vegetable broth in place of the chicken broth and swap in seitan or tempeh for the chicken.

PREP TIME 0:30 | COOK TIME 0:45

ingredients | Total Cost $19

2 tablespoons olive oil | Pantry

1 onion, chopped | $0.50

3 cloves garlic, chopped | Pantry

2 tablespoon chili powder | $1.50 for 1 ounce

1 teaspoon ground cumin | $1.50 for 1 ounce

$^1/_2$ teaspoon ground cinnamon | $1.50 for 1 ounce

1 (15 ounce) can diced tomatoes (preferably fire-roasted), with liquid | $2

1 yellow bell pepper, chopped | $0.50

2 canned chipotle peppers plus the adobo they are packed in, chopped | $1

1 14-ounces can chicken broth | $1

2 tablespoons (creamy) peanut butter | Pantry

2 ounces bittersweet chocolate, chopped | $3

1 small (2-3 pounds) roasting chicken, cut into pieces | $5

1 large yam or sweet potato, scrubbed and diced | $0.50

1 small bunch cilantro, chopped | $1

directions | Serves 4.

1. Heat oil in a deep soup pot over medium heat. Add onion and cook, stirring occasionally, until translucent. Add garlic and spices and continue to cook. Add diced tomatoes, yellow pepper, chipotle peppers, sweet potato, broth, peanut butter, and chocolate. Simmer for 10 minutes.

2. Add chicken pieces and use a spoon to ensure all chicken is covered by the liquid. Cook over medium-low heat for 35-45 minutes or until chicken is fully cooked (check by cutting into a large piece). Garnish with chopped cilantro.

oven-fried sriracha chicken

This chicken may look plain, but don't let its humble, golden-brown exterior fool you. For, beneath it's crunchy Panko coating, juicy, Sriracha-laced, buttermilk-marinated absurdly tender meat awaits.

Not to micromanage you or anything, but if, say, you were to take this chicken on a picnic, you might consider bringing along a light, crunchy Asian slaw and maybe some cold Peanut Noodles.

PREP TIME 0:15 (plus 2 hours marinating) | COOK TIME 0:30

ingredients | Total Cost $11.50

2 cups buttermilk | $1.50 for a pint

2 tablespoons soy sauce | Pantry

2 tablespoons (or more to taste) Sriracha, plus more for serving | $2 for 17 ounces

black pepper | Pantry

2 chicken thighs, bone-in, skin-intact | $2

2 chicken drumsticks, bone-in, skin-intact | $1.50

1 teaspoon salt | Pantry

2 cups Panko breadcrumbs | $3 for 16 ounces

1 egg, beaten | $1.50 for 12

vegetable oil in a spray bottle (or use nonstick cooking spray) | Pantry

directions | Serves 2–3

1. Whisk together the buttermilk, soy sauce, Sriracha, and 1 teaspoon black pepper. Transfer to an airtight container with a fitted lid (or use gallon-size zip-top plastic bag). Add the chicken pieces and toss gently to coat. Seal container (or bag). Marinate in the refrigerator for at least 2 hours (as long as overnight).

2. Preheat oven to 400°F. Line a baking sheet with foil and set aside.

3. Toss salt, Panko, and a few grinds of black pepper together in a mixing bowl.

4. To assemble, dip a piece of the marinated chicken in the egg, then transfer immediately to the Panko mixture. Use your hands to pat the Panko onto the chicken so it adheres. Place chicken on the foil-lined baking sheet. Repeat with remaining chicken and Panko.

5. Lightly spritz each chicken piece a few times with the oil, then bake for 25-30 minutes, or until juices run clear and chicken is golden-brown and crispy.

moroccan chicken with lemons, cranberries, and olives

This unique one-pot meal is perfect for company, but easy enough for a quiet night in. This is an ideal meal to cook a big batch of on Sunday night and then eat throughout the week. Look for inexpensive spices at your local Asian specialty store.

PREP TIME 0:25 | COOK TIME 0:40

ingredients | Total Cost $17

1 pound boneless, skinless chicken thighs, cut into 1-inch pieces | $3

salt and pepper | Pantry

2 tablespoons extra-virgin olive oil | Pantry

1 teaspoon cinnamon | $1.50 for 1 ounce

1 teaspoon paprika | $1.50 for 1 ounce

3 cloves garlic, chopped | Pantry

1 small piece ginger, peeled and minced | $0.50

3 tablespoons brown sugar | Pantry

2 Meyer lemons, sliced | $1.50

¹/₂ cup plain yogurt | $1.50 for 8 ounces

4 cups fresh spinach, cleaned and dried | $1

1 (12-ounce) jar pitted kalamata olives | $2

¹/₄ cup dried cranberries | $2.50 for 12 ounces

1 handful fresh cilantro leaves | $1 for a bunch

4 cups (cooked) Jasmine rice | $2 for 16 ounces

directions | Serves 3–4

1. Season chicken liberally with salt and pepper.

2. Heat olive oil in a large pot over medium heat. Add chicken and allow to brown lightly.

3. Stir in cinnamon, paprika, garlic, ginger, and brown sugar. Add lemons, yogurt, kalamata olives, yogurt, spinach, and $^2/_3$ cup water. Stir well. Cover and reduce heat to low. Cook 25-30 minutes, or until chicken is cooked through.

4. Remove $^1/_3$ mixture and transfer to a food processor. Pulse once or twice, just to lightly shred mixture (this can also be done with an immersion blender directly in the pot). Return to pot and stir well. Cook for 5 more minutes.

5. While chicken cooks, cook rice according to package directions.

6. Serve chicken mixture over rice. Garnish with chopped cilantro.

lamb tagine

Tagines were the original Crock-Pots—the very first "set-it-and-forget-it" appliances. Tagines (the name for both the stew and the dish it's cooked in) hail from Morocco, but their popularity now spans worldwide—and for good reason: cooking meat over low heat for long periods of time in flavorful spices and liquid yields a tender, aromatic result. The cone-shaped top on traditional tagines helps in this, promoting the return of all condensation to the bottom, allowing the stew's ingredients to cook evenly.

Don't worry if you don't have a tagine though—you can also cook this in a Dutch oven or other large pot with a fitted lid.

Note: Remember to buy your raisins and almonds in the bulk section for the best prices.

PREP TIME 0:30 | COOK TIME 2:30

ingredients | Total Cost $18.50

1 tablespoon vegetable or extra-virgin olive oil | Pantry

1 pound boneless lamb stew meat (cut into 1-inch pieces) | $7

1 red onion, halved and sliced | $0.50

2 cloves garlic, chopped | Pantry

1 (1 inch) piece ginger, peeled and grated | $0.50

1 red bell pepper, seeded and cut into 2-inch strips | $1

2 carrots, peeled and chopped into coin | $0.50

2 (15-ounce) cans diced tomatoes | $3

1/2 teaspoon ground cinnamon | $1.50 for 1 ounce

1/2 teaspoon ground turmeric | $1.50 for 1 ounce

3/4 teaspoon each of salt and pepper Pantry

1 tablespoon honey | Pantry

1/4 cup golden raisins | $1

1/4 cup blanched, slivered almonds | $1

1 handful fresh cilantro, chopped | $1 for a bunch

directions | Serves 4

1. Heat oil in a Dutch oven or tagine over medium-high heat. Brown the lamb on both sides, working in batches if necessary. Place browned meat on a clean plate and set aside.

2. Reduce heat to medium and add the onions and garlic to the pan (there should be enough fat left from the meat to cook them, but if not, add a touch more oil). Cook, stirring occasionally with a wooden spoon, until onions begin to wilt. Add the ginger, bell pepper, carrots, diced tomatoes, and $1/2$ cup water. Stir in the cinnamon, turmeric, salt, pepper, honey, and raisins.

3. Return the lamb to the mixture, stir well to combine, and cover. Reduce heat to medium-low and cook, undisturbed, for $2 \frac{1}{2}$ hours, or until lamb is very tender

4. Serve in bowls, plain, or over rice/couscous/quinoa, garnished with the almonds and chopped cilantro.

5. Other good toppings are harissa (or other hot sauce), plain yogurt and/or chopped Kalamata olives.

butter chicken

Whenever my friends and I go to our favorite Pakistani restaurant (Lahore Karahi, in San Francisco, CA), I always insist on this dish. In fact, if it were up to me, we could order nothing but this dish and I would be satisfied. A rich, buttery, and sweet tomato sauce covers incredibly tender chicken thighs. Occasionally, I'll throw in some chopped broccoli florets or fresh spinach, but more often I'll serve it plain, to better showcase its buttery deliciousness.

PREP TIME 0:50 | COOK TIME 0:45

ingredients | Total Cost $19

2 pounds boneless, skinless chicken thighs, chopped into 1-inch cubes | $3

4 garlic cloves, minced | Pantry

1 teaspoon curry powder | $1.50 for 1 ounce

1 teaspoon ground coriander | $1.50 for 1 ounce

2 teaspoons ground cumin | $1.50 for 1 ounce

1 teaspoon chili powder | $1.50 for 1 ounce

2 teaspoons ground cinnamon | $1.50 for 1 ounce

8 ounces Greek-style (thick) yogurt | $1.50

5 tablespoons butter | $1 for a stick

1 (6-ounce) can tomato paste | $1

1 (15-ounce) can chopped tomatoes | $1.50

1 tablespoon honey | Pantry

4 cardamom pods (crush pods slightly to release seeds and more flavor) | $1

1 cup heavy cream | $1.50 for a half-pint

1 teaspoon salt | Pantry

pepper to taste | Pantry

1 handful fresh cilantro or flat-leaf parsley, chopped | $1 for a bunch

directions | Serves 4

1. Combine chicken, garlic, spices (other than cardamom), and yogurt and mix well. Refrigerate in a covered container for at least 30 minutes (or as long as overnight).

2. In a heavy-bottomed pan over medium heat, melt butter. Add the tomato paste, chopped tomatoes, honey, and cardamom. Stir well. Bring to a light boil and reduce to medium-low to simmer, stirring occasionally, until sauce is thick (15-20 minutes).

3. Add chicken and cream and stir well. Continue to simmer for another 18-20 minutes, until chicken is fully cooked and very tender and sauce is creamy and thick.

4. Serve hot, garnished with cilantro or parsley.

chapter

9

afters

"Life is uncertain; eat dessert first," said writer Ernestine Ulmer, and I have to say, I tend to agree. Of course, eating dessert first might not always be practical, but just to be safe, I think it's a good idea to try to include it on a regular basis. Whether you're making two hundred Salted Fudge Brownies for a bake sale or a small batch of Brown Sugar Banana Spring Rolls to top off an intimate dinner for two, be sure to cook your desserts with plenty of love and to relish each bite. In these trying times, you'd be surprised at how far the comforts of a little sugar can go.

cinnamon-sugar doughnuts

These simple, classic cinnamon-sugar doughnuts are nothing more than lightly fried dough yet they taste very special. It's not necessary to deep fry them—an inch or so of vegetable oil in a deep frying pan or pot will do.

PREP TIME 0:15 | COOK TIME 0:03

ingredients | Total Cost $3

1 lb prepared pizza dough | $1.50

flour for dusting | Pantry

1/2 cup sugar | Pantry

1 tablespoon ground cinnamon | $1.50 for 1 ounce

vegetable oil for frying | Pantry

directions | Makes about 8 medium doughnuts and 8 doughnut holes

1. Gently roll the dough out into an 8 x 8-inch square on a lightly floured surface. Use a wine glass to cut as many 3-inch circles out of the dough as possible. Use a narrow shot glass or large thimble to cut out a smaller hole inside the circle so it looks like a doughnut (save the cut-out holes to make fried doughnut holes).

2. In a medium bowl mix the sugar and cinnamon until fully incorporated.

3. In a deep frying pan or pot, heat about 1 inch of vegetable oil over medium-high heat. Fry the doughnuts and doughnut holes two or three at a time for about one minute per side or until lightly golden brown. Using tongs, transfer the doughnuts and doughnut holes one at a time into the cinnamon-sugar mixture. Use your hands to coat well with the cinnamon-sugar and transfer to a plate. Repeat until all doughnuts and doughnut holes have been cooked and coated.

4. Serve hot with coffee or tea.

salted fudge brownies

Salted desserts are trendier than teen vampires right now, and with good reason. Flaky sea salt crystals enhance the chocolate's earthiness and balance its rich, sweet notes, resulting in a dessert that is not only more delicious, but more interesting to eat because it engages more of the palate. Serve these on their own or with a scoop of homemade ice cream.

PREP TIME 0:30 | COOK TIME 0:20

ingredients | Total Cost $14.50

³/₄ stick unsalted butter | $1 for a stick

4 ounces semi-sweet chocolate chips | $2 for a 12-ounce bag

¹/₈ cup unsweetened cocoa | $4 for 6 ounces

1 cup sugar | Pantry

1 egg | $1.50 for 6

1 teaspoon pure vanilla extract | $4 for 4 ounces

¹/₂ cup flour | Pantry

¹/₂ teaspoon coarse sea salt, plus more for sprinkling | $2 for 15 ounces

directions | Makes 8 brownies.

1. Preheat oven to 350°F. Lightly grease an 8 × 8-inch square pan. Set aside.

2. Fill a small saucepan about 2 inches high with tap water. Cover with a heat-proof bowl to create a double-boiler. Turn heat up to high and melt butter and chocolate chips in bowl, whisking frequently. Carefully remove bowl from pot and turn off heat.

3. Transfer melted chocolate and butter into a mixing bowl and whisk in cocoa, sugar, egg, vanilla, flour, and sea salt. Add about ¹/₂ cup water and whisk until mixture is very smooth.

4. Pour into prepared pan and bake 18-20 minutes or until top is shiny and few crumbs cling to an inserted toothpick.

5. Cool until the brownies are warm or room temperature. Cut into 8 squares and top each square with a few sea salt crystals.

thai iced tea cake

After three glasses of wine and about six chocolate chip cookies, my friend Andrew had the idea that I should make a dessert that incorporates the flavors of his favorite sweet drink, Thai iced tea. Despite having had a sufficient amount of wine and cookies myself, it was clear to me what a brilliant idea it was, so the following weekend, we baked a cake.

The sweetened condensed milk in the cake creates a lightly caramelized crust and the Thai tea gives it a beautiful bright orange color. This cake stayed on my mind for days to follow.

Note: look for the Thai tea at Asian specialty grocery stores.

PREP TIME 0:30 | COOK TIME 0:40

ingredients | Total Cost $12

1 stick unsalted butter | $1.50

¹/₂ cup loose-leaf Thai tea (cha-yen) | $3 for 12 ounces

1 tablespoon vanilla | $4 for 4 ounces

1 (6-ounce) can sweetened condensed milk, divided in half | $1.50

2 eggs | $1.50 for 6

¹/₂ teaspoon salt | Pantry

2 cups flour | Pantry

1 teaspoon baking powder | Pantry

¹/₂ cup powdered sugar | $1 for 16 ounces

directions | Serves 6–8

1. Preheat oven to 350°F. Use butter wrapper to grease an 8-inch loaf pan, 8-inch square cake pan, or 8-inch round cake pan.

2. Brew tea with ¾ cup boiling water, covered, for 10 minutes. Strain tea leaves and discard. In a mixing bowl, combine butter and freshly brewed tea until butter is completely melted. Whisk vanilla, half of the sweetened condensed milk, and the eggs. Mixture should be bright orange and very creamy. Gently stir in salt, flour, and baking powder. Pour into prepared pan and bake for 35-45 minutes or until a toothpick inserted into the center comes out clean. Allow cake to cool for 20 minutes.

3. While cake cools, make the glaze. Whisk together remaining sweetened condensed milk and powdered sugar until a thick, creamy mixture forms.

4. To serve cake, run a knife along the edge of the cooled cake to gently loosen it from its pan. Turn cake out onto a plate and drizzle glaze over the top, allowing it to run down the sides of the cake.

5. Cake can either be served immediately or chilled and served cold.

easy mini key lime pies

One of the coolest things about being a food blogger is that my friends frequently ask me for culinary help. My friend, James, for example, regularly calls to recite the contents of his refrigerator and ask what he can make from what is in front of him. I pretend to be annoyed, but secretly, I love helping.

So naturally, I was extra-excited when my friend Delia emailed me with a request for a Key lime pie recipe to make for her husband's upcoming birthday. I hadn't seen her in ten years, but thanks to Facebook, she was well informed that I can cook. I had never made Key lime pie before, but I'm always up for a challenge, so I set out to put together something fresh and homemade, yet simple and of course inexpensive. These were all of the above—not to mention delicious and refreshing. No worries if you can't find Key limes—regular limes make a fine substitute.

Note: If you want to skip the homemade crust, simply buy a pre-made graham cracker crust and make one pie instead of four miniature ones.

PREP TIME 0:30 | COOK TIME 0:15

ingredients | Total Cost $9

4 cups (about 1 box) Nilla Wafers, crushed until fine | $2.50 for a box

3 tablespoons flour | Pantry

1 stick unsalted butter, melted | $1

³/₄ cup sweetened-condensed milk | $2 for a 14-ounce can

5 ripe Key limes, juiced (about ¹/₂ cup) | $2

4 egg yolks, beaten | $1.50 for 6 eggs

directions | Makes one 8-inch pie or four mini pies

1. Preheat oven to 375°F. Lightly grease four (4-ounce) ramekins (or one 8-inch pie pan). Set aside

2. Combine crushed Nilla Wafers, flour, and butter. Stir until dough forms and is cohesive enough to handle. Wet hands with water and carefully press dough into prepared pan(s) to form a crust. Bake for 10-12 minutes or until lightly browned.

3. In a mixing bowl, whisk together the sweetened-condensed milk, lime juice, and egg yolks. Pour into prepared crusts and bake for 12-15 minutes, or until custard sets.

4. Cool completely and then refrigerate until serving.

SWEET, TART AND A LITTLE
BIT FLAKY, THESE ARE THE
TEEN POP STAR OF PASTRIES.

elliot's bananas in caramel sauce

Elliot, age eleven, is the older brother of Henry (inventor of the cheesy biscuits on page 40), and a dessert aficionado. He is not interested in the popsicles or packaged cookies, popular with his peers. No, Elliot prefers real, homemade desserts. Moreover, he likes making them with me. This is one of our favorites. We love watching how, in just minutes, plain old sugar, butter, and cream melt together to form an ooey-gooey caramel sauce, just perfect for ripe (but not soft—that is important) bananas. We like to eat this over vanilla ice cream or plain Greek yogurt with some toasted almonds sprinkled on top.

Elliot would like you to know that this sauce is also delicious with peaches, pears, or apples. We haven't tried berries yet, but that would probably be good, too.

PREP TIME 0:05 | COOK TIME 0:15

ingredients | Total Cost $3

2 tablespoons unsalted butter | $1 for a stick

²/₃ cup sugar | Pantry

pinch of salt | Pantry

³/₄ cup heavy whipping cream | $1.50 for a half-pint

2 ripe but still-firm bananas, peeled and sliced into ¹/₂-thick slices | $0.50

directions | Serves 2-4.

1. In a medium frying pan over medium heat, melt the butter and swirl it all over the pan.

2. Sprinkle the sugar and salt over the melted butter and stir gently. It should look like wet sand. Cook this mixture, stirring very occasionally, until it begins to melt. As it melts, scrape the sides of the pan down, using a rubber scraper. Continue doing this until the mixture is completely melted.

3. Gently whisk the mixture while you pour in the cream. Let it melt, then start stirring again. Continue cooking until you have a creamy, golden-brown caramel sauce.

4. Add the sliced bananas and arrange in the pan so they are submerged. Cook for 1-2 minutes, just until bananas have softened. Remove from heat.

5. Let cool for 2-3 minutes, then serve over ice cream (preferably vanilla).

dessert quesadillas

Every year, my mom insists on giving my brother and me foil-wrapped milk chocolate Santas at Christmastime . . . and every year he and I exchange knowing glances because we both know that our respective chocolate St. Nicks will sit on our respective coffee tables for a few weeks until we get tired of looking at them and they end up dying their inevitable respective deaths in our respective compost bins.

I was just about to toss this year's ridiculous Lindt Santa when it occurred to me that I could use it to make the dessert tortillas I dreamed up a few weeks ago—and actually, it was perfect. The milky chocolate fused perfectly with the cream cheese and cinnamon, making the whole thing taste like a blend of warm chocolate ganache, cheesecake, and churros—all in about 15 minutes.

PREP TIME 0:08 | COOK TIME 0:08

ingredients | Total Cost $8

4 (8-inch) flour tortillas | $3 for 24

4 ounces cream cheese | $1.50 for 8 ounces

4 ounces milk chocolate chips or chunks | $2 for 14 ounces

few dashes of cinnamon | $1.50 for 1 ounce

few dashes of salt | Pantry

2 tablespoons unsalted butter, divided | $1 for a stick

directions | Serves 4

1. Heat oven to 200°.

2. Spread each tortilla with an ounce of cream cheese.

3. Sprinkle the chocolate pieces over half of the tortilla, on top of the cream cheese. Top with a dash each of salt and cinnamon and fold over to make a half-moon.

4. Heat ½ tablespoon of butter in a medium frying pan over medium heat and cook the quesadilla on both sides, until the chocolate is melted and the tortilla is golden-brown. Transfer to an ungreased baking sheet and keep warm in the preheated oven until ready to serve. Continue cooking with remaining butter and quesadillas (using ½ tablespoon for each quesadilla).

5. Cut into wedges and serve warm, garnished with powdered sugar if desired.

peanut butter-corn flake treats

One day, in the spirit of waste-not-want-not, I decided to use up the aging corn flakes that were sitting in my pantry.

I'm not a huge fan of corn flakes with milk for breakfast but these easy rice crispy treat stand-ins are addictive (and vegan too!).

Note: If you have other cereal in your pantry, feel free to use it in place. These would be delicious with granola, raisin bran, or even Cap'n Crunch.

PREP TIME 0:25 | COOK TIME 0:05

ingredients | Total Cost $5

vegetable oil or cooking spray for greasing pan | Pantry

¼ cup shredded coconut | $2 for 12 ounces

1½ cups brown sugar | Pantry

½ cup honey | Pantry

1 cup peanut butter (creamy or crunchy) | Pantry

4 cups corn flakes | $3 for a 12-ounce box

directions | Serves 6–8

1. Lightly grease an 8 × 8 square pan. Set aside.
2. Toast coconut in a dry skillet over medium-high heat. Set aside.
3. In a large pot over medium-high heat, stir together brown sugar, honey, peanut butter, and 2 tablespoons water until peanut butter melts and mixture begins to bubble. Remove from heat.
4. Stir in corn flakes and toasted coconut until completely mixed.
5. Use wet hands to carefully pack warm cornflake mixture into prepared pan.
6. Allow to cool for 30-60 minutes.
7. Cut into squares and serve.

baked apples

These baked apples are a refreshing twist on a classic dish. I like to make them when I'm expecting company because they make the entire house smell amazing.

PREP TIME 0:10 | COOK TIME 0:30

ingredients | Total Cost $4.50

2 Fuji, Gala, or Granny Smith apples | $1

2 tablespoons unsalted butter, cut into small pieces | $1 for a stick

2 tablespoons sour cream | $1.50

1 (1-inch) piece of ginger, peeled and minced | $1

1/8 cup sugar | Pantry

directions | Makes 2 baked apples

1. Preheat oven to 375°F.

2. Cut off the top of each apple, about 1 inch down. Set aside.

3. Use a paring knife to scoop out the cores of the apples, creating a hole about 2 inches deep and 2 inches wide in each apple. Carefully cut about 1/8 inch off of the bottoms of the apples so that each apple has a flat base.

4. In a small bowl, whisk together the butter, sour cream, ginger, and sugar. Divide evenly between the apples and pack into the hollow centers. Replace the apple tops and bake for 30 minutes or until the apples have softened and the skin crinkles.

salted chocolate chip cookies

I've never had much of a taste for revenge, but once, after he ruined a beautiful batch of risotto by spitting a half-eaten, bright red cinnamon candy into it as it simmered, I made my little brother a batch of salt pancakes (please note that we were nine and twelve years old). The gullible, risotto-destroying little brat saw nothing amiss in the golden stack of flapjacks presented to him by his big sis, and so he took a huge buttery, syrup-drenched bite. Of course, the cup-and-a-half of Morton I had poured into the batter made his lips curl into a look of disgust before he spat out the half-chewed sodium bomb.

So when he called while I was testing this recipe and I told him what I was doing, he laughed and said, "You would add unnecessary salt to something delicious. Thank you for being transparent with your intentions this time."

I promise you this, dear reader: My days of intentionally ruining sweet dishes with copious amounts of salt have gone the way of slap bracelets, Full House, and not getting along with my little brother. Now, I only add salt to foods to make them extra delicious. Trust me on this one.

PREP TIME 0:15 | COOK TIME 0:12

ingredients | Total Cost $9.50

1 stick unsalted butter, at room temperature) | $1

1¼ cups firmly-packed brown sugar | Pantry

1 tablespoon pure vanilla extract | $4 for 4 ounces

1 large egg | $1.50 for 12

1¾ cups all-purpose flour | Pantry

½ teaspoon salt | Pantry

¾ teaspoon baking soda | Pantry

1 cup semi-sweet chocolate chips (1 6-ounce package) | $3 for 12 oz.

3 teaspoons coarse sea salt or Kosher salt | $1.50 for 4.5 ounces

directions | Makes about 30 cookies

1. Preheat oven to 350°F. Lightly grease a baking sheet and set aside.

2. Beat together using a whisk, electric mixer, or stand-up mixer the butter, brown sugar, vanilla, and egg until fluffy.

3. Mix together the flour, salt, and baking soda in a separate bowl.

4. Stir the flour mixture into the butter mixture, taking care not to over-mix. Gently fold in the chocolate chips.

5. Working in batches, drop the dough by rounded tablespoons onto the prepared baking sheet, making sure there are at least 2 inches between each dough ball.

6. Bake for approximately 8 minutes, until the cookies have begun to brown on the bottom but are still soft on top. Remove baking sheet from oven, and put a small pinch of the coarse salt on top of each cookie and press down gently, to embed them slightly. Bake for another 4-6 minutes, or until cookies are golden-brown.

7. Let cool for at least 5 minutes before serving.

s'mores-style rice krispies treats

One night, while hanging out with two of my favorite children, a serious conflict arose: one child wanted s'mores for dessert, the other had his heart set on Rice Krispy Treats.

Before a heated argument could ensue, I insisted they come up with a compromise. This recipe was the result.

PREP TIME 0:20 | COOK TIME 0:04

ingredients | Total Cost $9.50

6 graham crackers | $2.50 for a box of 40

1 package (about 40) regular marshmallows or 4 cups miniature marshmallows | $2.50

3 tablespoons unsalted butter | $1 for a stick

5 cups crispy rice cereal | $2.50 for a box

½ cup semisweet chocolate chips | $2 for 8 ounces

directions | Serves 8–10

1. Line a 13 x 9 baking pan with parchment or wax paper (it may also be greased with butter). Set aside.

2. Place the graham crackers in a zip-top plastic bag and use a wine bottle or rolling pin to crush into medium crumbs. Set aside.

3. Place the marshmallows and butter in a large pot over medium-low heat. Stir continuously as they melt together. Once the mixture is very gooey with no lumps, remove from heat (this may also be done in the microwave).

4. Scrape the marshmallow mixture into a large mixing bowl. Add the graham cracker crumbs and crispy rice cereal and stir well.

5. Once combined, stir in the chocolate chips, just until distributed.

6. Scrape the mixture into the prepared pan and wet your hands slightly with cool water (this prevents sticking). Use your hands to press the mixture into the pan.

7. Let cool for at least 20 minutes (preferably at least an hour) before cutting into squares and serving.

brown sugar-peach semifreddos

Semifreddos are just the thing when you want to serve a special frozen dessert but don't have an ice cream maker. Here, the brown sugar imparts a unique caramel flavor to the fresh peach custard, making these truly memorable. Serve with a sprig of mint and maybe a few fresh raspberries.

PREP TIME 3:00 | COOK TIME 0:20

ingredients | Total Cost $8.50

6 ripe peaches, peeled, diced | $4

1 pint half-and-half | $1.50

1 cup brown sugar | Pantry

3 egg yolks, lightly beaten | $1.50 for 6 eggs

pinch salt | Pantry

9 foil muffin cup liners | $1.50 for 50

directions | Makes 9 semifreddos

1. Using a blender or food processor, puree half of the diced peaches. Set aside.

2. In a medium pot, heat half-and-half and brown sugar over medium heat, whisking until steamy (but not boiling).

3. Pour about $1/2$ cup warm half-and-half mixture into the egg yolks and whisk to mix. Slowly add the egg mixture to the half-and-half mixture, whisking constantly. Add the salt. Continue whisking until a custard thick enough to coat the back of a spoon forms.

4. Pour custard into a bowl and allow to cool (refrigerating helps) for 30 minutes.

5. Add peach puree and diced peaches to cooled custard. Set aside.

6. Line 9 regular muffin cups with foil liners. Carefully pour the peach-custard mixture into the muffin cups.

7. Freeze for at least 2 hours, or until needed.

cranberry-zinfandel brownie bites

These were born when I had half of a bottle of Zinfandel left over from the night before and dark chocolate on the mind, after attending a chocolate-tasting party at a friend's house. Hence, I did the thing that made sense: I combined the two, studded the result with plump dried cranberries and popped it in the oven. Winey, chocolaty bliss.

Feel free to serve these with, um, more zinfandel—or a good port.

PREP TIME 0:30 | COOK TIME 0:18

ingredients | Total Cost $13

³/₄ **(6 tablespoons) stick unsalted butter, plus more for greasing pan** | $1 for a stick

²/₃ **cup inexpensive Zinfandel** | $2.50 for a bottle

4 ounces semi-sweet chocolate chips | $2 for a 12-ounce bag

¹/₈ **cup unsweetened cocoa** | $4 for 6 ounces

1 cup sugar | Pantry

1 egg | $1.50 for 12

³/₄ **cup flour** | Pantry

¹/₂ **teaspoon salt** | Pantry

¹/₄ **cup dried cranberries** | $2

directions | Makes 12 mini brownie bites or 8–10 square brownies

1. Preheat oven to 350°F. Lightly butter a 12-cup mini-cupcake tray or an 8 × 8-inch square pan. Set aside.

2. Combine the butter and wine in a small saucepan and cook over medium-high heat for 6-8 minutes, stirring constantly, until butter melts and wine has reduced. Reduce heat to medium, add chocolate chips, and whisk gently until chocolate melts.

3. Transfer melted chocolate-butter-wine mixture to a mixing bowl and whisk in cocoa, sugar, egg, flour, and salt. Add about ⅛ cup water and whisk until mixture is very smooth.

4. Pour into prepared muffin cups/pan and top each muffin cup (every 2 ½ inches if you're using an 8 x 8-inch pan) with a few cranberries. Bake 15-18 minutes or until top is shiny and few crumbs cling to an inserted toothpick.

5. Cool until the brownies are warm or room temperature and carefully remove from muffin cups (or cut into squares).

brown sugar-banana spring rolls

This is one of those desserts that impresses everyone—and for good reason. These spring rolls are sophisticated-looking and bursting with flavor . . . so don't bother telling anyone that they were ridiculously easy to make and cost you almost nothing. Just bask in their praise and thank me later.

PREP TIME 0:10 | COOK TIME 0:10

ingredients | Total Cost $5

1 banana | $0.50

4 large egg roll wrappers | $2

4 tablespoons shredded coconut | $1

4 tablespoons brown sugar | Pantry

cinnamon | $1.50 for 1 ounce

vegetable oil | Pantry

directions | Makes 4 spring rolls

1. Slice the banana into fourths lengthwise so you have four long pieces of banana. Slice the long pieces in half so you have eight short, thin pieces of banana.

2. Lay a wonton wrapper on a clean, dry surface. Make a little mound with 1 tablespoon of coconut and 1 tablespoon of brown sugar in the center of the wrap. Lay 2 banana slices on top of the mound, sprinkle a dash of cinnamon on the banana and roll up, tucking in the ends of the wrapper, as though making a little burrito. Repeat with the remaining wontons.

3. Heat about an inch of oil in a medium frying pan over high heat. Cook the spring rolls for 1-2 minutes on each side until golden brown and crisp. Drain on paper towels.

4. Serve sliced on the bias, garnished with a little more cinnamon.

chardonnay-poached pears

When it comes to sexy food, there are established aphrodisiacs and then there are the foods that, for whatever reason, we as individuals are particularly responsive to. For me, this is it. The pears become lusciously spoon-soft after a long bath in chardonnay and honey, and the balsamic wakes up the taste buds as it brings out the tartness of the raspberry preserves. I don't make this for people I'm not hoping to make out with.

PREP TIME 0:10 | COOK TIME 1:00

ingredients | Total Cost $5.50

2 Bosc pears | $1

½ bottle inexpensive Chardonnay | $2.50

1 tablespoon honey | Pantry

2 tablespoons sugar | Pantry

3 tablespoons raspberry preserves (buy a small jar of store brand) | $2

1 tablespoon balsamic vinegar | Pantry

directions | Serves 2

1. Peel pears and set aside. In a medium pot, whisk together wine and honey. Add pears and bring to a boil. Reduce heat to a simmer and allow to cook covered for 45 minutes (this is a good time to eat your dinner). Once pears are cooked to the point that they could be easily pierced by a fork, remove using a slotted spoon and set aside. Leave wine mixture in pot, turn up heat, bringing the wine to a boil, and whisk in the sugar, raspberry jam, and balsamic vinegar until dissolved. Stir constantly for several minutes until mixture reduces to a syrupy consistency. Serve pears in small bowls on top of a little pool of the raspberry-balsamic reduction.

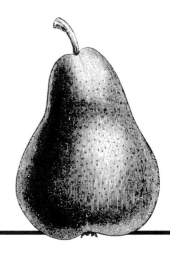

the brokeass pumpkin-spice latte

Ahh, Fall. Season of color-changing leaves, crisp mornings, and the eponymous pumpkin-spice latte.

It's an oft-yearned-for treat when September finally comes around and local coffee shops finally roll out their strictly seasonal pumpkin-flavored coffee drinks. But if you're buying them daily or even every other day, at nearly $4 a pop, it can add up to a lot of dough to be plunking down for coffee infused with what is essentially nutmeg-scented, artificially-colored-and-flavored high-fructose corn syrup.

But don't worry, there is a BrokeAss solution: make them at home with high-quality ingredients, obviously. This freshly brewed, wildly cheap version of the pumpkin-spice latte can be warming your hands and your spirits any time you please—even after the coffee shops close, and without an espresso machine. The directions below are for one latte, but the ingredients priced out will make about a week's worth of homemade lattes. And best yet, you likely have most (if not all) of the ingredients at home already. If you like your lattes straight, feel free to omit the spices and/or sweetener.

PREP TIME 0:10 | COOK TIME: 0:010 (10 seconds)

ingredients | Total Cost $10.50 (ingredients listed are enough to make about ten lattes)

3 tablespoons strong ground coffee | $6 for 16 ounces

²⁄₃ cup water

¹⁄₂ teaspoon pumpkin pie spice | $1.50 for 1 ounce

2 teaspoons honey or agave nectar | Pantry

²⁄₃ cup milk (any fat percentage, or even soy) | $3 for a gallon

directions | Serves 1

1. Brew the coffee with the water in a regular coffee maker, French press, or drip cone.

2. While the coffee brews, stir the pumpkin pie spice into the honey or agave nectar until completely blended. Set aside.

3. Pour the cold milk into a microwave-safe bowl, the edges of which should come up a bit higher than the milk.

4. Keep the bowl slightly tilted to the side, so that the milk is gathered more toward one side. Using a wire whisk, quickly and vigorously whisk the milk in the bowl for about 2-2¹⁄₂ minutes. If milk is not frothy after 2¹⁄₂ minutes, continue whisking an additional 30-60 seconds. The milk should be very frothy at this point.

5. Microwave the milk in the bowl on high for 8-10 seconds. It should puff into a high foam immediately.

6. To serve the latte, pour the hot coffee into a mug and stir in the honey/agave-spice mixture until completely dissolved. Top with the hot milk, spooning the thick foam on top. A dash of additional pumpkin pie spice or some ground cinnamon on top is a nice touch. Serve immediately.

chapter
10

last words

menu ideas

a romantic meal for two

Happy Heart Salads, Truffled Mac and Cheese, Grilled Lamb Chops over Carrot-Gorgonzola Smash, Chardonnay-Poached Pears, Crisp Rose or Sangiovese

weekend bbq

Vietnamese Veggie Spring Rolls with Peanut Sauce, Guacamole and tortilla chips, Pico de Gallo, Cashew-Bulgur Veggie Burgers, BBQ Pork Burgers, fresh watermelon, S'mores Rice Krispy Treats, beer, sodas, lemonade.

superbowl (or project runway) sunday

Pepperoni Pizza Spirals, Brown Sugar Sriracha Hot Wings, Easy Molasses Pulled-Pork Sandwiches, chips, veggies, White Bean Dip, torn pita, Brown Sugar-Banana Spring Rolls, beer, soda.

comfort food night

Caesar Salad, Brown Butter-Pumpkin Mac and Cheese, Henry's Cheesy Biscuits, Third-Date Chicken, Sriracha-Glazed Carrots, Baked Apples, Pinot Noir, apple cider.

una buena fiesta

Guacamole, Pico de Gallo, tortilla chips, Beer Battered Fish Tacos, Chicken and Sweet Potato Mole, Dessert Quesadillas, beer, margaritas.

nine wines for $10 or less

When my friend, Adam Metz, and I started the BrokeAss Gourmet website together back in 2009, we spent several nights a week (after working our full-time day jobs all day) drafting recipes, Skyping with our designer, and writing pitches. As for nourishment, the agreement was I'd cook and he would provide the wine. As such, he became quite gifted at selecting tasty budget wines and, so, below you'll find his list.

Hint: A cheap wine aerator (available at most kitchen supply stores, Target, or WalMart) will make even the cheapest wines taste better.

One more thing: If you don't have access to a Trader Joe's, where some of the cheapest good wines can be found, try ordering from any of these great websites:

Grand Wine Cellar: http://www.grandwinecellar.com/

The Wine Library: http://www.winelibrary.com

Joe Canal's http://www.joecanals.com/

Beverages and More: http://www.bevmo.com

Shopper's Vineyard: http://www.shoppersvineyard.com

the whites:

1. **Honey Moon Viognier** | ($5)
   This is an excellent low-priced white these days, and it drinks as well as many $20 Viogniers, at $\frac{1}{4}$ the price.

2. **2007 Gaetano d'Aquino Orvieto Classico** | ($5)
   A dry Italian white, perfect for a light pasta or fish supper.

3. **2003 Fuerza Malbec** | ($4)
   An excellent white at an excellent price point. Goes with almost anything.

4. **2004 or 2003 Screw Kappa Napa Chardonnay** | ($9–$10)
   Although the price of this Sebastiani bad boy has certainly increased a little since its release, this is still a keeper, and in the right price range.

5. **Charles Shaw Blush Zin** | ($2)
   Possibly the best sangria wine available. Aerate a couple of bottles with an immersion blender (or even in your regular blender) and mix. Just get a case, and prepare for summer (slowly).

the reds:

1. **2006 Bogle Zin (or 2007)** | $10 or $8
   This one tastes way fancier than the price point would lead you to believe. Pair it with turkey meatballs, veggie burritos, or any rich entree.

2. **Red Truck Merlot** | ($9–$10)
   This Sonoma all-American is just fine for a weeknight. Excellent with burgers or a BrokeAss flank steak.

3. **Cycles Gladiator 2005 Central Coast Merlot** | ($8–$10)
   Cycles calls this one "the wine to drink while you wait for your Cabernet to age." There are worse ways to bide your time.

4. **Charles Shaw Cab** | ($2)
   Buy this one by the case, and aerate before using. A rock-solid Monday night wine, but try to avoid drinking the whole bottle yourself, as the tannins can be a little annoying after awhile.

5 non-brokeass splurges that are worth it

If you're cooking and eating at home, rather than going out to eat on a regular basis, chances are you can afford the occasional splurge. Below you'll find five items that I believe are truly worth it. Buy them when you can, use them with an awareness that they cost more than your regular purchases, but enjoy every bite. That is, after all, the whole point of all this, right?

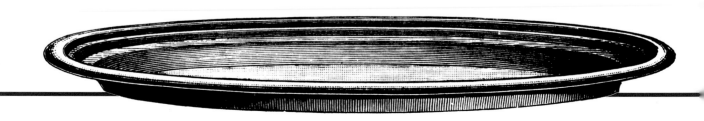

- **Pastured Eggs** | $6–$7.50

  If you're lucky enough to live near an egg farm, try to buy your eggs directly from there. Otherwise check out your local farmers' market or natural foods store for eggs that are not just organic and free range, but actually pasture-raised. Be warned: A dozen of these delicious beauties can cost up to $7.50, but the difference in their flavor is remarkable. While pastured eggs are perhaps not a good choice for baking, whip up an omelet, scramble, or breakfast sandwich using one of these and you'll taste the difference in their rich, dark orange yolk and creamy whites.

- **Muir Glen Organic Fire-Roasted Tomatoes (Crushed, Diced and Sauce)** | $2.50–$4

  These are, hands down, the best canned tomatoes money can buy. Stir them into a rich stew or Indian dish, or cook them with fresh garlic, extra virgin olive oil, basil, salt, and pepper for an impromptu tomato sauce. However you use them, they impart a charred-yet-sweet addition to whatever you're making, adding layers of flavor in an instant. Sometimes it's cheaper to buy them online through Amazon.

- **Kerrygold Irish Butter** | $2–$3

  This rich, deep-yellow, European-style butter is imported from Ireland, made from 100 percent grass-fed cows and is literally the best butter money can buy, in my opinion. I don't use it for baking, but I'll happily cook eggs in a dab of it, serve it with crusty bread for spreading, or melt it over steamed vegetables. It's an effortless (and not too costly) way to kick a dish up several notches in the decadence department.

- **Good, Cold-Pressed Extra-Virgin Olive Oil** | $6–$12+

  Good cooking techniques will take you far, but a dish is truly only as good as the quality of its ingredients. I use an inexpensive extra-virgin olive oil (always buy extra virgin—"pure" or "light" olive oils are useless) for baking/sauteeing , but any time I want the flavor of the oil to shine through (in dressings/sauces, for example), I use something with good flavor. Two options that won't break the bank: Trader Joe's California Extra-Virgin Olive Oil (in a slim green bottle), $5.99 and Whole Foods 365 brand Extra Virgin Cold-Pressed Italian Olive Oil (in a cylindrical tin), $8.99.

- **Organic Free-Range Chicken, Grass-Fed Meats, and Wild-Caught Fish** | prices vary

  It can be painful, whilst standing at the meat and/or seafood counter at the grocery store to bring yourself to spend several additional dollars per pound on sustainably raised meats/seafood, but when flavor and quality count, it truly is better this way. I'm not saying it's imperative to always do this (these are splurges, remember), but when you can afford it, this is the way to go. Buy only what you need (the biggest key to BrokeAss shopping) and augment your meal with plenty of fresh (and less-expensive) vegetables and/or other sides.

fun (and savings) at your local farmers market

I'm often asked for insider tips on how to save money while food shopping. I always recommend Trader Joe's for pantry basics. An herb garden is a wonderful and inexpensive way to have fresh herbs on hand and a CSA box split between friends can be an affordable way to access fresh, locally grown produce. But for my money (and time), nothing beats a friendly-vendor-and-music-filled visit to my local farmers' market.

Many people think that shopping at a farmers' market is more expensive than buying at a grocery store. Well, sometimes that might be true, but I've found that with just a little bit of thought and planning, you can find great deals on fresh, often organic goods—all while supporting your local community and having quite a really good time. Just follow my guidelines:

Bring your own bags. Obviously you do this already (and if you don't, you should be!), but beyond reusing big plastic grocery bags or bringing a tote, consider saving and reusing plastic produce bags, too. Many vendors now charge $0.25 and up for new ones.

Show up late. In my experience, showing up at my farmers' market during its final hour has many benefits. First of all, the crowd has begun to clear out, so there is less of a wait at vendors' stalls and it's easier to cruising the aisles. More important, most vendors are eager to get rid of their goods and so will either lower their starting prices or be willing to bargain. I recently bought two generously filled cartons of figs for $3, down from $4 a piece, because I arrived at the fig stand just as they were closing. Obviously, I was psyched. You know how I feel about figs.

Buy meat, fish, eggs, and dairy in smaller quantities. If I weren't on a budget, I would buy 100 percent of my meat, fish, eggs and dairy at the farmers' market. But given the name of this book and what I'm trying to do here, obviously, I'm watching my wallet. I still partake in the deliciousness of such products available, I just do so sparingly. A special cheese, a six-pack of farm-fresh eggs, a small package of sausages—it can all be done on limited funds. Just choose wisely.

Go consistently and befriend vendors. I once got a huge bag of poblano chilies for free. Yes, free. The purveyor at one of my favorite vegetable stands thinks I'm charming—and he appreciates that I show up every week to buy from him. He almost always throws in a little extra something for me when I stop by, and never fails to cut me a great deal. Kindness and loyalty count at the farmers' market—and as my grandfather always said, it doesn't cost anything to be nice.

If farmers' market shopping isn't already a part of your life, I encourage you to incorporate it. If you don't know where the market closest to you is, look up your city on the USDA website (http://search.ams.usda.gov/farmersmarkets/) or check your local newspaper for listings. Saving money always feels good, especially when you can support your community's agriculture and local economy at the same time.